People in low-paid informal work

'Need not greed'

People in low-paid informal work

'Need not greed'

Dennis Katungi, Emma Neale and Aaron Barbour

First published in Great Britain in June 2006 by

The Policy Press
Fourth Floor, Beacon House
Queen's Road
Bristol BS8 1QU
UK

Tel no +44 (0)117 331 4054
Fax no +44 (0)117 331 4093
Email tpp-info@bristol.ac.uk
www.policypress.org.uk

Published for the Joseph Rowntree Foundation by The Policy Press

ISBN-10 1 86134 892 4
ISBN-13 978 1 86134 892 0

British Library Cataloguing in Publication Data
A catalogue record for this book is available from the British Library.

Library of Congress Cataloging-in-Publication Data
A catalog record for this book has been requested.

Dennis Katungi, Emma Neale and **Aaron Barbour** are members of Link UK, the national arm of Community Links.

The **Joseph Rowntree Foundation** has supported this project as part of its programme of research and innovative development projects, which it hopes will be of value to policy makers, practitioners and service users. The facts presented and views expressed in this report are, however, those of the authors and not necessarily those of the Foundation.

The statements and opinions contained within this publication are solely those of the authors and not of The University of Bristol or The Policy Press. The University of Bristol and The Policy Press disclaim responsibility for any injury to persons or property resulting from any material published in this publication.

The Policy Press works to counter discrimination on grounds of gender, race, disability, age and sexuality.

Cover design by Qube Design Associates, Bristol
Printed in Great Britain by Latimer Trend Printing Group, Plymouth

Contents

Preface   vii
Acknowledgements   viii
Executive summary   ix

1   Introduction   **1**

2   Policy context and introduction to the research findings   **3**
Poverty in the UK   4
Wider policy relevance   4
Introduction to the research findings   5

3   Informal work as a response to poverty   **7**
Low wages   7
Low benefit levels   8
Those who cannot undertake formal work   8
Safety net   9
Costs of childcare   9
Housing costs   10
The asylum process   11
Foreign students   12
Complex issues   12
Surviving   13
Striving   13
Choice and constraint   13

4   Sidestepping barriers to formal paid work   **15**
Barriers to formal paid work   15
The informal and formal job search process   17
Social networks   17
Availability of low-paid informal work   18
Attraction of informal work   19
The employer–employee relationship   20
Benefits of informal paid work   22

5   Informal work as a response to crisis   **23**
Financial crisis   23
Fear of debt   24
Family breakdown   24
Job search in times of crisis   24

6   Attitudes to low-paid informal work: towards a typology   **25**
Unaware of the law   25
Informal paid work as a norm   26
Aware of the law, but preferring to work   26
Aware of the law, but justifying informal work   27
'Turning a blind eye'   28

7   Experiences of low-paid informal work: case studies   **29**
      Case Study One: Rasheed   29
      Case Study Two: Joe   30
      Case Study Three: Naomi   30
      Case Study Four: Saira   31
      Case Study Five: Jane   32
      Case Study Six: Margaret   33

8   Overview of current policy   **34**
      Supportive, not punitive, policy   34
      Tax Credits   34
      Childcare element   35
      Welfare to work   36
      Benefits   36
      Support for small businesses   37
      Deterrence   37

9   Policy recommendations   **38**
      Overview   38
      Changing attitudes and approaches   38
      Affordable living   39
      Changing rules and systems   40
      Extend the Housing Benefit run-on   41
      Harnessing hidden potential   45
      Information and education   47
      Further research   48

10 Conclusion   **50**

      References   51
      Appendix A: Research methodology   54
      Appendix B: Overview of core research area: London Borough of Newham   58
      Appendix C: Community Links and the Community Links 'What if...?' Team   60

Preface

Community Links

Our vision is to be champions of social change.

Our purpose is to tackle the causes and consequences of social exclusion by developing and running first-rate practical activities in East London, and by sharing the local experience with practitioners and policy makers nationwide.

We live our values. We strive simply:

'To generate change. To tackle causes not symptoms, find solutions not palliatives. To recognise that we need to give as well as to receive and to appreciate that those who experience a problem understand it best. To act local but think global, teach but never stop learning. To distinguish between the diversity that enriches society and the inequalities that diminish it. To grow – but above all to build a network not an empire. To be driven by dreams, judged on delivery. To never do things for people but to guide and support, to train and enable, to simply inspire'.

Community Links is an innovative inner city charity running community-based projects in East London. Founded in 1977, we now help over 53,000 vulnerable children, young people and adults every year, with most of our work delivered in the London Borough of Newham, one of the poorest boroughs in Europe. Practical ideas making life easier and better: new thinking, challenging perceptions and raising the bar. Our successes influence both community-based organisations nationwide and government policy.

Community Links and the informal economy

Over the last five years Community Links has taken a particular interest in the informal economic activity of small businesses, the self-employed, and presented in this report, employees. Why? Because the informal economy has such a huge impact on the lives of the people with whom we work, and plays such an integral role in their experience of poverty.

We are committed to continue to tackle the causes and find solutions to overcome poverty; and share our learning nationally with decision and policy makers. This report makes a valuable contribution to this end, and adds to our growing body of work about the informal economy. Most recently we have developed a new methodology to quantify informal economic activity at a borough-wide level, the first of its kind in Europe.

We now plan, with our partners, to develop, pilot and evaluate a number of practical projects, which will support people in deprived areas to make the transition from informal to formal paid work.

You can join us by becoming a member of the national informal economy network of cross-sector organisations and individuals which will promote policy and practice changes.

For further details please contact www.community-links.org or email uk@community-links.org

Acknowledgements

We gratefully acknowledge the support and funding for this research by the Joseph Rowntree Foundation. We are especially thankful for the keen interest of Helen Barnard at JRF.

Thank you to the hard work of the Project Advisory Group. Their insights and guidance have been invaluable:

Geraldine Blake	LinksUK
Chris Burgess	Federation of Small Businesses and
	Business Solutions
Miriam Kajungu	Local resident
Janet Murungi	Hackney Women's Project
Izzie O'Hara, Roger Halson and Liz Longden	Her Majesty's Revenue and Customs
Matthew Smerdon	The Baring Foundation and Community Links
Erika Watson	Prowess
Professor Colin Williams	University of Leicester Management Centre

Thank you to the LinksUK team at Community Links including:

Zoraida Colorado
Richard McKeever
David Robinson

A special thanks to the volunteer community researchers. Their efforts contributed enormously in carrying this project to a successful conclusion:

Charity Aheebwa	Naila Imran
Hughie Ashman	Matilda Olango
Patricia Costa	Erick Owoahene

And Clarissa White, formerly of BMRB, and now of The National Centre for Social Research (NatCen), for the very practical and supportive training for our volunteer community researchers.

Finally, a big thank you to the people who came forward with their stories.

Executive summary

This report explores the experience of people on low incomes, in informal paid work, including those working cash-in-hand and those undertaking undeclared work while claiming benefits. Informal paid work is defined as work that 'involves the paid production and sale of goods or services which are unregistered by, or hidden from the state for tax, benefit and/or labour law purposes, but which are legal in all other respects' (SBC, 2004, p 9). The UK informal economy is estimated to be worth around £75 billion annually (SBC, 2004).

The research presented in this report used qualitative methods (see Appendix A). Participants were recruited to reflect a wide range of characteristics. One hundred people were interviewed face to face. Four focus groups were held with local service providers and policy makers. The research was carried out in the London Borough of Newham (see Appendix B). The recommendations are based not only on this research but also on Community Links' experience as a support agency and service provider in East London and on previous research and policy work.

The context of low-paid informal work

Informal work is undertaken in response to poverty

The research finds that informal work is undertaken by people who live in poverty, who fear going without basics such as food and heating or are facing mounting rent arrears. This issue should be opened to public debate with a focus on creating an environment that enables people to leave low-paid informal work and supports those who have few rights because they are informally employed.

Government initiatives could go further

A clear cross-government policy is needed to deal with the issue of low-paid informal work, with a view to helping those who wish to make the transition to formal employment, or helping those who are employed informally and who have few rights. There is a need for more effective, targeted employment training and skills development; strategies to combat families becoming entrenched in low-paid informal work to tackle child poverty; welfare and tax reform based on an understanding of why people work informally; changes to the asylum system; and local-level responses.

Harnessing potential

Informal paid work continues to be regarded as fraud and therefore as a matter of enforcement by government. Punitive measures employed to 'tackle' this activity have limited success where poverty drives the decision to work informally. There is much to gain from developing strategies towards informal work that take into consideration people's level of need and access to opportunities, and regard people as untapped potential within the economy.

Poverty as a driver of informal work

Poverty was at the root of much of the informal work examined in this study. Some participants felt that the alternative to taking up informal paid work was absolute material poverty – not having enough income to pay for food and bills. Others undertook informal paid work as a route out of poverty.

Low wages and low benefit levels

There were three basic issues that underpinned most of the informal working found in this study: low benefit rates, low wages and rules that limited the hours that people can work. The problems caused by low wages and benefits were exacerbated by a number of factors, discussed below.

Informal work due to high costs of childcare and housing

Participants stated that high rents and the costs of childcare presented a major barrier to formal employment. Those in rented and temporary accommodation reported that if they worked formally they would lose Housing Benefit, and be left with inadequate income for basic needs. Some parents were able to save the costs of childcare as they took their children with them to informal jobs.

Informal work in times of crises

Debt was a key reason given for taking up informal employment. In 2004, 6.1 million families had difficulties in meeting their debt repayments (FSA, 2004). Participants also turned to informal work in response to a sudden change in family circumstances. At these times of crisis, being caught for fraud seemed a less threatening prospect than the immediate risks of being without food, heating or being threatened by debt collectors.

The tax and benefit system

Participants reported that the tax and benefit system created disincentives to returning to work. In particular, fears about inefficiencies in the system made participants wary of building up arrears while waiting for run-on or reinstated payments on returning to work. Participants also observed that they would be no better off when working formally, due to losing linked benefits.

Informal job search networks

The process of finding a job informally was faster and easier than looking for formal work. Informal work was found to relate to the types of networks which participants were part of, and those which they tended to be excluded from. Participants finding informal work through social networks could avoid the costs associated with formal recruitment processes, such as writing application forms, travel and time for interviews. Some participants also found confidence a barrier to formal job search and preferred to find work through friends and family.

Flexibility among employers

Participants reported that informal employers could be more flexible around working arrangements to fit in with their individual circumstances. Some participants with particular health needs found that formal employers were inflexible around hospital appointments and illness and therefore turned to informal work, retaining benefits for security. A number of parents spoke of taking up low-paid informal work to fit around new childcare responsibilities. They felt that informal work that could fit around childcare times was more available.

Barriers to formal work

Participants identified a range of barriers to formal work. Participants identified more informal than formal opportunities for people with few skills and qualifications, or with qualifications that are not recognised in the UK. Perceptions of discrimination based on age, health, ethnicity and (incorrect) assumptions about illegal residence among formal employers were also identified.

Bridging work

Informal work was also undertaken by people who were not able, or were not yet ready, to work for many hours but who wanted to keep in touch with the world of work. They could not do enough work to support themselves (and therefore needed to maintain their benefits) but did want to do more voluntary, part-time or occasional work than the system allowed for.

Employer responsibility

Participants felt that some agencies were happy to accept people with fraudulent paperwork due to critical staff shortages in some areas. Certain industries may be identified where informal working is particularly common, such as the construction industry and cleaning services. Large reputable establishments may indirectly use low-paid informal work. Participants reported that some employers say that employees are self-employed to absolve themselves of responsibility.

Voluntary and community sector employers

Participants spoke of a blurred line between employees and volunteers, with organisations wanting to pay volunteers for their work when they could afford to. This had to be informal so that people could carry on claiming benefits as it was not necessarily possible to pay them all the time or at levels that would allow them to survive without benefits.

Employer–employee relationship

Some participants noted that employers were exploitative, requiring long hours and offering little pay. The study suggests that a relationship with an informal employer may be at once exploitative and supportive. Some participants spoke of support and assistance from their employers in making the transition to formal employment, such as providing work experience and references.

Towards a typology: attitudes to low-paid informal work

A typology begins to emerge from the attitudes of the interviewees towards low-paid informal work. Lister's (2005) research into poverty in the UK suggests a typology of reactions to poverty. This includes 'getting by', 'getting back at', 'getting out' and 'getting organised', that is, people who struggle to get by every day; those who use strategies of everyday resistance; those who use strategies to get out of poverty; and those who join together to effect wider change.

This research identified the following categories among informal employees: those unaware of the law; those for whom informal working is a norm; those preferring to work rather than claim; and those justifying their informal activity. Some participants saw informal work as a norm, within their family, among friends or in their locality. Some young people thought that the cash-in-hand work they were doing that was over the tax threshold was legal, when in fact they should have been paying taxes.

Other respondents were aware of the law but preferred to work than to do nothing. These people did not consider benefits an option, preferring to do low-paid informal work rather than claim benefits. Participants identified a type of person who justified their informal work. There was a sense of informal paid work providing a kind of social justice.

The benefits of informal paid work

Employers using informal workers enabled participants who faced barriers to formal work to access employment. They also helped people to find temporary solutions to crisis. Participants' stories indicate a range of individual benefits, including increased confidence, skills and work experience, and potential pathways into formal work.

There are also potentially family, community and social benefits from informal work, including increased social cohesion (Pfau-Effinger, 2003). The people who work in informal paid work are in themselves a potential resource to the economy as a whole. They are people who want to work and have skills and abilities.

Summary of recommendations

Changing attitudes and approaches

The research findings about the informal economy indicate that a fundamental change of approach is needed across the spectrum of welfare policy. National and local floor targets around helping people who wish to move from the informal to the formal economy may help to engender this.

In order for policy change to be successfully embedded, public and institutional attitudes must support this change. Rather than making informal paid work less socially acceptable, as suggested in the Grabiner (2000) report, the emphasis should be on promoting understanding of informal work as a response to poverty.

Need not greed

Policy and practice that deal with people who work informally should acknowledge the idea that everyone has a right to survive. If there are no accessible alternatives, then people may reasonably be expected to support themselves and their families through informal paid work. Measures should aim to help people who work informally to survive, to offer 'carrots', real routes out of poverty through formal working, while addressing some of the other issues affecting their lives, including housing, debt, skills, training and childcare.

Systems and rules

Reform of the tax system

- *Simplify the tax system:* the tax system should not force people to choose between survival and informality. Either very low incomes should not be taxed, or the first band of one's personal tax allowance should

rise. The benefits and tax threshold should be coordinated more closely, to smooth the transition from receiving benefits to progressing through a 'no benefits, no tax' point to paying tax.
- *Create a supportive tax system:* some work, currently considered informal, could be brought into the formal sphere through tax breaks for organisations or individuals. In addition, voluntary sector organisations should be allowed to employ people who are in receipt of benefits, on a casual basis, in work that benefits the local community.
- *Reform the Tax Credit system:* the Tax Credit system remains an area in need of reform and simplification. Tax rebates or exemption from PAYE for those on the minimum wage might be considered. Including more parents within the Tax Credits system by changing thresholds for Tax Credits and excluding Tax Credits as income in the calculation for entitlement to Housing Benefit would reduce the numbers of people working and claiming.

Reform of the benefits system

- *Simplify the benefits system:* the benefits system is overly complicated and a careful and systematic reassessment is needed (NAO, 2005).
- *Raise benefit levels:* benefits should be raised to allow people to cover basic living costs. Current levels of income, such as £55 a week for a single person on Jobseeker's Allowance, do not cover basic living costs.
- *Revise Housing Benefit rules:* consideration should be given to extending the Housing Benefit run-on with a taper to enable people to come off this benefit slowly.
- *Uncouple benefits:* currently, on losing Income Support, all passport-ed benefits such as Housing Benefit, Council Tax, free prescriptions and school meals, are lost. Uncoupling benefits would reduce the disincentive to take formal jobs.
- *Raise the Earnings Disregard:* levels of the Earnings Disregard, the amount of money one can earn while in receipt of benefits, which have remained unchanged since 1988, should be raised and index-linked, enabling people on benefits to take part-time or sessional jobs.
- *Avert administrative error:* the current separation between Revenue & Customs and

the benefits agencies means that it is relatively easy for administrative error to occur in the payment of state benefits. Linkages could show a person's situation and therefore eligibility for benefits. Greater database unification would also facilitate smooth transition from benefits to work and could respond immediately to changes and keep the right balance between benefits and tax, guaranteeing a basic income.

- *Provide better staff training:* a clear understanding of policy by frontline delivery staff, to inform people of their entitlement and to reduce error, is needed to underpin this. A system sensitive to residents' needs should recognise different types of diversity, including the different understanding of other countries' systems.

Improving systems for recently arrived workers

- *Improve the asylum system:* people seeking asylum should have the right to work and the asylum process should be made more efficient. Genuine refugees wait for years before they are permitted to work due to delays in the process. During this time, people are expected to live on National Asylum Support Service (NASS) vouchers worth 70% of Income Support.
- *Publicise National Insurance number laws:* delays in the process of applying for a National Insurance number should be reduced and the rules should be clarified and more widely publicised. There is a need to inform and educate employers and employees about the legal situation.

Harnessing potential

Employers

- *Increase the National Minimum Wage:* Raising, indexing and enforcing the minimum wage may help to divert people from low-paid informal work.
- *Tailor support:* so that it is as easy to find formal job opportunities as it is to find informal ones. This may include, for example, using outreach workers to disseminate news about formal job opportunities into communities known to have high levels of informal working.
- *Create routes into work:* The initiative should be taken by employers, government

agencies and the voluntary and community sector to improve access to formal jobs, and to include work with recruitment agencies on reaching out to those in informal work. New types of work experience, volunteering opportunities and internships with the voluntary sector and with business that are flexible to the needs and timetables of individuals should be explored.

- *Provide adequate childcare provision:* lack of childcare is a major barrier to formal employment. Informal flexible working is the only option for some. The solution is seen partly to lie in the generic provision of childcare and partly family-friendly employment policies.

Corporate social responsibility

- *Target specific industries:* Industries known to employ more people in informal work should be targeted, to support these employees to create more economically viable formal opportunities. Achieving this in construction and domestic consumer services would deal with 85% of all informal work (SBC, 2004).
- *Support small employers:* small businesses should be supported to move employees into legitimacy.
- *Make available better formal paid work options:* for people in deprived areas to win people over from the informal sector. 'Making work pay' is not just about the wage rate and in-work benefits, it is also about offering security of tenure, job progression and good, supportive working environments. It is vital that there are more part-time or sessional jobs that can fit around caring responsibilities or health needs.
- *Alleviate debt:* Measures relating to financial inclusion and education could be implemented to avert people from working informally when they face times of financial crisis; for example, a further tightening of the consumer credit regulations, support for people to build their savings and assets, and staggered and deferred debt repayment for people leaving benefits.

National information campaign

- A national information campaign should be delivered to raise awareness of the advantages of formal work, the disadvantages of informal work and the role of the tax and benefits systems.

- A range of methods including non-traditional techniques should be used to reach those people who may be harder to access. These may include using nationwide networks of community groups to help disseminate information about benefits and signpost support.

Further research

More research is needed in order to understand the complex issues that lead people into the informal economy. The development of a firm evidence base should include the analysis of practical pilots. Research could focus on the following:

- informal employers: taking a closer look at the informal economy from the perspective of employers;
- background, culture and informal employment: looking at people's experience and understanding of work from a cross-country perspective;
- routes out of the informal economy: talking to people who have made the transition into the formal economy;
- how money earned informally is spent and the impact of the informally earned cash on the local area;
- the impact of housing costs on informal working;
- the role of sub-contracting in the informal economy;
- a survey of attitudes of children and young people on informal working.

Pilot projects

An initiative equivalent to 'Pathfinders to Work', testing ways in which people can be supported to make the transition from informal to formal paid work, could be established. Pilots suggested by this research include the following:

- *Specialised 'informal economy' transition and support teams* should be set up by Revenue & Customs and the Department for Work and Pensions, throughout the regions, to advise and support individuals who are in low-paid informal work, to protect their rights and enable voluntary transition to formal work without fear of judgement or punishment. These teams should also offer support to those who wish to remain in informal paid work until they are ready, as well as to those who wish to move into formal work.
- *A school curriculum module* on the world of work including the benefits of formal working and the tax and benefit system should be developed that could be adapted to be locally relevant. It would be equally important to ensure that teachers know of the potential benefits of selecting this module within personal, health and social education lessons to begin with, but move towards making this a core subject.

Introduction

This report explores the experience of people on low incomes and in informal work, including both those working cash-in-hand and those undertaking undeclared work whilst claiming benefits. The report sets out the role that informal paid work plays in the lives of people who have low incomes and live in poverty. It provides policy makers with a greater understanding of the choices that people on low incomes and in poverty are making and how government policy and practice can better respond to these.

The 'informal economy' is known by a host of names: the hidden economy, cash-in-hand work, moonlighting, the grey economy, working off the books, tax evasion and benefit fraud. Within this report we have adopted the definition used by the Small Business Council (SBC, 2004, p 9): 'Informal work involves the paid production and sale of goods or services which are unregistered by, or hidden from the state for tax, benefit and/or labour law purposes, but which are legal in all other respects'. This definition excludes the criminal element of the informal economy such as drug dealing, prostitution or gun running. In this report, we also exclude self-employment, provisioning and mutual aid, in order to focus on the experience of employees.

A considerable number of people in the UK have played a part in the informal economy. The European Union (EU) estimates that the informal economy accounted for 7-16% of GDP in the European economic area in the 1990s (Williams and Windebank, 2004a), equating to around £75 billion of the UK's economy (SBC, 2004).

In the UK and Europe, research on the informal economy is concerned with its illegality and devising ways to reduce and prevent such activity. For example, much of the research conducted by the Joint Research Centre of the European Commission Employment and Social Affairs into 'undeclared work' takes such a stance (Renooy et al, 2001). However, there is increasing recognition that some people work in informal paid work through perceived necessity and lack of other opportunities, and not through choice, and would like to work in formal paid work, or to leave benefits, and 'go legit', if they could.

This report is based on qualitative face-to-face interviews with 100 London Borough of Newham residents conducted between November 2004 and August 2005. Four follow-up focus groups were carried out with 20 frontline staff and policymakers. The work also builds on wider research and on the practice knowledge of Community Links Advice Team staff. The Community Links 'What if...?' Team set out to establish a snapshot of employees in low-paid informal work in Newham; their circumstances, motivations, wages, awareness of government programmes, their benefit situations, personal barriers to formal employment and finally, their aspirations and ideas for solutions.

It was felt that a qualitative approach would be the most appropriate methodology given the sensitivities that surround engaging in informal paid work and the need to assure interviewees of utmost confidentiality. The research is qualitative and makes no assertions about the extent of informal activity among people on low incomes. Rather, it looks at the variety of reasons and attitudes presented by participants in this situation. This type of exploratory qualitative research is a necessary precursor to building an understanding of the scale of the issues through quantitative methods. The Community Links 'What If...?' Team have subsequently been commissioned to carry out research to quantify the informal economy in the London Boroughs of Newham and Haringey.

The sample included people currently or recently in low-paid informal work, widely spread across ethnicity, gender and age. A 'snowball' or chain referral method of recruitment was applied. The methodology is set out in detail in Appendix A. The 100 interviewees all live or work in the London Borough of Newham. Newham provides a case study of a deprived city borough. It ranks among the most deprived areas in the UK, graded 11th most deprived on the Index of Multiple Deprivation. Research suggests that preconditions for the existence of low-paid informal work are likely to vary geographically. However, many of the factors found in this report to lead participants to informal rather than formal paid work will be found across deprived areas, and in pockets within more affluent areas.

Further characteristics of Newham are detailed in Appendix B. Previous research shows that the availability of informal work opportunities to people in low-income jobs varies from area to area. In certain areas people on low incomes do not have access to informal or formal opportunities, while those on higher incomes may have access to both. A discussion of these issues can be found in the book *On the margins of exclusion* (Smith, 2005).

This research intends to provide foundations for developing practical pilot projects aimed at helping those in low-paid informal work to make the transition to formal employment. The recommendations (in Chapter 9) highlight the changes in benefits, taxation, asylum policy, education and other areas that would create a situation in which people in low-paid informal work could make this transition more easily.

Policy context and introduction to the research findings

Existing research suggests that the informal economy is increasingly recognised as a global phenomenon. The informal economy has grown relative to the formal economy across advanced market economies, in Central and Eastern Europe, and in the developing world (ILO, 2002). Williams and Windebank (2004a) argue that the informal economy is much more complex than the stereotypical view of low-paid workers in sweat shops; it includes a wide range of activity from small businesses through to community work. The informal labour market is segmented, so some jobs are poorly paid and have few rights, and others enjoy much better conditions and pay.

European Union (EU) informal economic activity is particularly prevalent in the service industries, including seasonal agricultural work. European Union ascension has enabled workers to move across borders, to fill low-paid service sector jobs by undercutting wage levels. Other factors acting as drivers of the informal economy range from processes of globalisation, increased sub-contracting, outsourcing and variations in employment contracts. These are all part of a context of increasing flexibility, which is generating a more segmented labour market, within which marginalised groups, largely in deprived neighbourhoods, play a specific role.

White and blue collar informal economic activity in the financial services, IT, and personal services, is reported across the EU. Skilled workers are more likely to obtain informal employment through existing networks in the workplace, than the stereotypical benefit claimant or immigrant 'working for cash-in-hand'. And it is mainly marginalised people, particularly women and members of minority ethnic communities, who are prone to exploitation in the informal economy because of unequal employment opportunities (Williams and Windebank, 1998, 2004a).

The informal economy has recently received increased attention from the UK government and media, including images of exploited cockle pickers, and more recently a focus on people working while claiming benefits. A discussion of approaches to low-paid informal work from different government departments can be found in Chapter 8.

In September 2003, Community Links and Street (UK) hosted a senior inspector from the Cross-Cutting Policy Team of Her Majesty's Revenue & Customs (HMRC) for six months. As a result, HMRC has a new central compliance team, including a unit focusing specifically on the informal economy. A cross-government working group has been established to coordinate work on the informal economy.

Many theorists now give credence to the idea that those in informal paid work are an economic asset and that policy initiatives should be aimed at bringing them into the legitimate sphere (ILO, 2002; SBC, 2004; Williams and Windebank, 2004b). However, where people are on low incomes and face poverty, this presents a particular challenge.

Poverty in the UK

This study examines the relationship between poverty and informal work. The research encountered self-reported absolute poverty where people go without basic needs, and also relative poverty. In addition, poverty of opportunity was identified as a driver encouraging people to undertake informal paid work and child poverty emerged as a key driver.

A commonly used measure of relative poverty is those living on less than 60% of median disposable income, adjusted for family size. This amounts to £98 per week for a single person with no children, £182 for a lone parent with two children (aged five and 11) and £210 for a couple with one young child. 'Better-off' calculations, offered by the job centre and advice services, to show how much more an individual would earn in employment, suggest that faced with low wage levels, some people would be no better off financially in work than they would be on benefits. According to this measure, one in four people in the UK, or nearly 13 million people, live in poverty (BOND et al, 2005).

The United Nations Development Programme defines poverty more widely, as the lack of ability to live a long, healthy and creative life; to be knowledgeable, and to enjoy a decent standard of living; to enjoy dignity, self-respect, and the respect of others. It sees a 'life of respect and value' as a key aim of human development. For some participants in this study, informal paid work gave them these things; the opportunity to strive as well as to survive.

The Labour Party manifesto (2005) pledged to end child poverty, starting by halving it – both in terms of relative low income and in terms of material deprivation – by 2010-11. A raft of government initiatives, such as Sure Start and Tax Credits are in progress to try to change the fortunes of families with children. This is a significant task as 3.5 million or more children in the UK still live below the poverty line (New Policy Institute, 2005). Government targets for reducing child poverty by 25% between 1998/99 to 2004/05 according to the households below average income measure have not been met. Also, the situations of the poorest, those with below 40% of average income, have not been improved (Brewer et al, 2006). This research indicates that assisting those in low-paid informal work could be a useful addition to existing strategies. People trapped in low-paid informal work to support their families and keep them out of poverty in the short term, may miss opportunities to progress to better jobs and step out of poverty in the longer term.

Wider policy relevance

The research findings set out in this report indicate that low-paid informal work is an issue that cuts across the spectrum of local and central government concerns. A broad look at government policy indicates that the current agendas relating to low-paid informal work include: targeting employment training and skills to job opportunities; appropriate and not punitive welfare reform; increasing the potential for local government to work with the issue of informal paid work; and creating stronger social cohesion.

Employment and training

The Labour Party manifesto (2005) declares a belief in equality, dignity and opportunity for all and that work is the best anti-poverty strategy. In addition to a commitment to full employment, the government pledges to go further and move people from 'low to high skilled employment', and provide 'better rewards and conditions for all'. This research suggests that government policy and instruments for tackling employment are not currently designed to reach out to people who are in informal work, to improve their prospects. Observation of the tax and welfare system suggests that there is opportunity for change through developing appropriate indicators and floor targets to measure success in promoting gainful employment for those in low-paid informal work and improving the Tax Credit regime.

Welfare reform

The Welfare Reform Green Paper issued in January 2006 (DWP, 2006), reviews the rationale of the benefits system, including considerations of incentives to work. This research suggests that there is potential to hone the theoretical understanding of the choices that people make by including consideration of the option of informal paid work. The report also finds a great potential to improve the design and delivery of welfare services by engaging with the idea that people may work informally to top-up low benefits and wages. The issue is particularly pertinent in view of the proposed reform of Incapacity Benefit. Housing costs and Housing Benefit also pose problems which, this research suggests, encourage informal work.

Social cohesion

The government acknowledges that wasted potential for employment can have a negative impact on social cohesion. The government 'Respect' agenda puts neighbourhoods and neighbourliness high on the political agenda. In addition, the informal economy is a key issue in considering the settling and inclusion of newcomers to the UK. Where informal work is low paid and mundane, and fails to protect workers' rights or provide opportunities for advancement, it can be said to be wasting potential. On the other hand, it is argued that informal paid work can contribute to social cohesion (Pfau-Effinger, 2003).

Local government

The programme of reform set out in the White Paper on modernising local government finance in March 2001, gives local authorities increased control over local regeneration budgets, employment and deprivation (DTLR, 2001). This report suggests that the dynamic of low-paid informal work at a local level should be seen as key to understanding these issues.

Introduction to the research findings

Chapters 3 to 8 present a qualitative analysis of interviews with people employed in low-paid informal work. They look at personal circumstances and responses to them, as well as experiences of the benefits, tax and asylum systems. They suggest the need for new approaches and methods to support people who wish to make the transition to formal paid work and to assist those who may not yet be ready to do so.

The report to the Treasury on the informal economy by Lord Grabiner QC (Grabiner, 2000) acknowledges that there are people in informal paid work and businesses who would like to make the transition into the formal sphere, but face barriers to doing so: 'Some of those in the informal economy would like to come clean. But they may not know what opportunities exist in the regular economy or how to take advantage of them. It is important to take steps to encourage these people and their businesses to become legitimate' (Grabiner, 2000, p 5).

This research finds that while the barriers to moving from informal to formal paid work include lack of knowledge or awareness, they are much more wide-ranging than this. The many reasons why people start to work in the informal economy include the fear of, or to pay off, debt, poverty, childcare and asylum issues and the types of work available. These factors all contribute to an 'informal paid work trap'. A clearer understanding of what these barriers to leaving informal paid work are can lead to a much more effective programme of assistance and support. In the words of one interviewee:

> 'Informal paid work is not the problem to tackle; it is what makes it tick. If these conditions of low pay, asylum seekers with no right to work, and families with young children who can't work because they couldn't afford childcare are not tackled, then informal paid work would be impossible to tackle...' (Erick, 30)[1]

---

[1] All names have been changed to protect participants' identities.

3

Informal work as a response to poverty

This chapter sets out some of the reasons participants gave for working cash-in-hand or working while claiming benefits. The research presents the experiences of participants who are on low incomes, and facing poverty. Different kinds/levels of poverty were encountered in the course of this research. Other studies of informal work suggest that it can be a response to poverty: 'While it may be seen as a way of circumventing state regulations, [informal work] clearly provides people with work strategies that ensure reasonable living conditions' (Vasta, 2004, p 6). 'Working off-the-cards is a form of survival strategy for those who needed to supplement their benefit income' (North et al, 2004, p 9).

There were many reasons for participants in this study taking up informal work, but poverty was the underlying theme. Participants saw no way of earning a living and supporting themselves and their families other than through low-paid informal work. Some felt that the alternative was absolute material poverty – not having enough income to pay for shelter, food and bills. Other participants undertook informal paid work to save up for a better life; or for important life events such as weddings.

Low wages

Some interviewees in low-wage jobs worked informally in a second job, to top up their formal income. The main issues cited were not being able to afford childcare costs, lack of flexibility in formal employment and high housing costs. In theory, the Tax Credit system should make those on lower incomes better off and remove the need for low-paid workers to do this. However, there are a range of reasons why, despite this system, Tax Credits do not work for everyone on low incomes (explored further in Chapter 8).

The Living Wage Unit highlights the low wages earned by some Londoners. A recent study of workers on low incomes in London found average gross earnings across typical low-paid sectors to be £5.45 an hour, less than half the average salary nationally, and a third of the average salary for London (Evans et al, 2005). The Greater London Authority estimates a 'Living Wage' for London, which would cover minimum living costs, at £6.70 an hour. Including Tax Credits, Housing Benefit and Council Tax Benefit, the wage level to keep people above the poverty line would give an income of £8.10 per hour (GLA, 2005). Research suggests that in particular locations, low benefits levels and deregulated labour markets 'encourage resort to unreported work to get by' (Lister, 2005, p 139). People from minority ethnic groups in particular face low wages. Holgate (2005) states that 'many in these groups find themselves in low-paid, low-skilled jobs primarily because of their ethnicity and regardless of their skills and qualifications'.

The weekly income for a single person over the age of 24 with no dependants on Jobseeker's Allowance is £57.45 (2006-07 rates) and, in addition to this, that person recoups the cost of their rent through Housing Benefit, provided the accommodation size and price is assessed to be fair. The weekly wage for full-time work at the minimum wage including Tax Credits for this person would be £115.50, with approximately £35 paid towards the rent from Housing Benefit payment and approximately £10 paid towards council tax. Assuming that weekly rent for a one-bedroom flat in the private rented sector is £95 per week, the choice would be between:

• Benefits: weekly income after housing costs = £57.45
• Working: weekly income after housing costs = £ 45.50

Even with Tax Credits, these income levels would leave them no better off than if they were on basic benefits, with £57.45 on benefits and £45.50 working full time. This is well below the poverty line, which is £98 per week for a single person with no children (BOND et al, 2005). In formal paid work the person would also lose other linked benefits. While someone returning to work may receive a back-to-work incentive, such as bonus of up to £1,000 for benefits lost (CAB, 2005), in the longer term the prospect of taking work may not be attractive. Detailed calculations of living costs show that on the minimum wage, after all deductions, £20 disposable income is available; and that on Income Support or Jobseeker's Allowance, necessary weekly expenditure exceeds income by £30.[2]

Low benefit levels

Some research participants perceived benefit levels to be insufficient for survival. Research indicates that those living on basic benefits may face the choice of incurring debt or cutting back on essentials for day-to-day living (Kempson, 1996). Some research participants responded to this choice by taking up informal paid work. With the benefits as a safety net, and another income to provide a little extra money, the alternative of an insecure and low-paid job seemed less attractive to them.

> 'I wonder how they arrive at the sum of £56.20 as money that is enough for a 31-year-old to live on in a week. It means that whoever is on this allowance has to find other ways to make ends meet, hence cash-in-hand work.' (Kassim, 31)

> 'People don't leap into full-time low-paid work unless it is going to change their situations for the better. In the case of those in informal paid work, it normally doesn't suit them because their coping mechanism of topping up benefits has already kicked in and they see this as a better alternative to poverty in work.' (Welfare worker)

> 'All I can say is that people around here are poor. Taking informal paid work is their way of doing something about poverty. They try to make their lives and that of their families a little better by earning a bit on the side. Living on benefits alone is living in poverty.' (Phillip, 58)

Those who cannot undertake formal work

The Trades Union Congress (BOND et al, 2005) points to the fact that many children in poverty have parents who cannot always work in regular jobs. They may be disabled or

---

[2] www.york.ac.uk/res/fbu/documents/LCAsingleman2005.pdf

sick or a lone parent without childcare. For these families, benefits are essential, and insufficient. Other studies report barriers to work faced by those coming off Incapacity Benefit (Dorsett et al, 1998). In the present study, some research participants on Incapacity Benefit or Disability Living Allowance who did not feel confident enough to go into full-time work for health or disability reasons preferred to claim benefits and take flexible informal paid work. In situations where they could be well and working in one week and unwell the next, work with some kind of flexibility was more suitable. Some concern that support to work is not enough for some people has been expressed: 'While we welcome extra support and assistance to help more lone parents and disabled people into employment, it's not an easy fix for those with high barriers to entering the jobs market' (CPAG, 2006; response to Welfare Reform Green Paper). Respondents also reported that some informal employers could be more flexible about taking time off, or arranging working hours or weekly rotas around individual needs. Respondents spoke of frustration at the failure of formal employers to accommodate health needs.

'I had a medical problem and needed to go to hospital for tests and appointments. This became very difficult as my employer did not want to give me the time off. If I had a more senior position this would not have been a problem because I noticed they took time off as and when they needed to without it being an issue. I applied for about eight jobs unsuccessfully before I found this one.' (Suzanne, 56)

Safety net

The Office of the Deputy Prime Minister (SEU, 2004, p 39) acknowledges that one factor keeping people from formal employment is the 'fear of the risks involved in the transition to work compared to the relative security of benefits'.One reason why participants with health issues or childcare needs chose not to declare work while on benefits was that they feared losing their formal jobs as a result of their illness or caring responsibilities. For others, the work in itself was temporary or seasonal. These participants feared that delays in the benefits system would leave them in difficulty if they declared and then lost their work. Smith (2005, p 156) finds that 'for cash workers, undeclared work and welfare benefits can serve as an insurance against insecurity in the formal labour market'. While 'Rapid Reclaim', introduced in the 2000 Budget, entitles people to take short-term contracts and return to benefits, advice staff report that a lack of system efficiency in local benefits offices causes delays and errors, which may put people off the idea of coming on and off benefits. The 2006 Welfare Reform Green Paper (DWP, 2006, p 100) states that 'the biggest barrier to taking up a new job for those on benefits is the fear of the unknown and of falling foul of the benefits system'.

'Our boss employs four other boys apart from me. This work is not reliable, you may be busy for a few weeks and then work dries up, you can't go off benefits just because you've got a bit of work like this, it's very hard to get back benefits once you lose them.' (Amos, 22)

'I got a student to move in with me, I resumed my chambermaid evening shifts to four times a week. She stayed with the kids and I managed to do my cash-in-hand work, this gave me £120 per week on top of benefits and the student stayed with us rent free. During holidays she would go away and I would not be able to work. If I told Benefits people about this income, they would just cut me off benefits, and because I know I can't do without them, I take the risk not to tell them.' (Martha, 38, lone parent with four children)

Costs of childcare

High childcare costs mean that many parents need to top-up low wages or benefits in order to pay them. Participants felt that if they worked in formal full-time employment they would lose much of their income in childcare costs, even with Child Tax Credits. They felt that they would be better off if they looked after their own children and fitted flexible work around this, and that they would see something of their children. The work they found that could accommodate them was informal.

> 'Childcare is a big issue. The cost of placing a baby like ours with a registered childminder, if my wife got a job, is £200 per week. Unregistered childcare is available for half that price or less. It is their own arrangements. I don't see how government interventions with Child Tax Credits can be effective unless they provide universal childcare.' (Iqbal, 29)

Some parents felt that moving off benefits to take up full-time formal employment would leave their families destitute. Other studies have identified that 'those who undertake unreported work often justify it with reference to family responsibilities' (Lister, 2005, p 139).

> 'I get £600 per month Income Support, £400 per month Housing Benefit, and £75 Council Tax Benefit, which totals £1,075 per month. If I add what I earn cash-in-hand – £400 per month – that's £1,475 per month. With no qualifications, work experience or even references since I have never worked formally, do you think I would get a job to pay me that amount? How would I manage with the kids anyway? In this job I work when I can, and they understand my situation.' (Jackie, 28, lone parent with two children, works for cash-in-hand as a hairdresser)

Lone parents in particular do not have the option of one parent staying at home. Some chose to work nights in flexible informal work and look after their children in the day, rather than take on a formal job with conventional hours. Respondents reported that the supply of flexible jobs in the area tended to be informal.

Housing costs

Some participants stated that the main factor compelling them to undertake informal paid work was the cost of their housing and the need to keep their Housing Benefit. Community Links Benefits Advisers suggest that the fact that Tax Credits count as earnings and are deductible from Housing Benefit makes the prospect of taking low-paid work even less attractive. Lack of affordable housing, high rents, shortages of housing and space and living in temporary accommodation are widespread, particularly in London.

Respondents in temporary accommodation in particular stressed that these rent levels create a major disincentive to taking up formal employment. Experience indicates that people in temporary accommodation often remain socially excluded because high rents prevent them from being able to find work (ALG, 2004). For every pound a tenant in temporary accommodation earns formally, they lose 65 pence in Housing Benefit under the benefit 'taper' rules (Wolk and Foster, 2003). Rent levels for temporary accommodation, in rural and inner-city areas, are set by councils above market rates. Officially the average stay in temporary housing in the Newham area lasts for two years, however anecdotal evidence from local advice workers suggests that people are likely to wait for seven years, or even up to 10 years before they can move to permanent accommodation.

'Juliet was in full-time work and staying with parents, but because she was expecting a child, she was placed in temporary accommodation by the local authority. She then had to downgrade to part-time work because she would not be able to afford the rent of £360 per week had she remained in a full-time role. To become eligible for Housing Benefit she changed from 35 to 15 hours of work per week. She then started to work informally looking after children for £100 per week to make up for lost income and to 'make ends meet'. (Juliet's mother, Kellen, 46)

The asylum process

Those asylum seekers who are eligible for support are given vouchers from the National Asylum Support Service (NASS) which can be exchanged for items such as grocery provisions. NASS vouchers for adults are equivalent to 70% of basic Income Support, around £40 per week. NASS vouchers for children are currently around £38 per week. Respondents felt that this amount was insufficient to live on and therefore took on informal work to survive.

'My husband went to the Home Office to apply for a work permit so that he could start work because we had been here for two-and-a-half years waiting for Home Office to decide on our asylum, but he was turned down and officials asked why he wanted a work permit when he was on NASS support. From there he got informal paid work as a barber because we and the kids were living in abject poverty. By the time we got leave to remain, both my husband and I were doing cash-in-hand work and we still do'. (Christine, 28)

This finding is supported by research for Oxfam and the Refugee Council into living on NASS support: 'Organisations working with asylum-seekers remain deeply concerned that, even with NASS payments, the level of support to asylum-seekers is set so low ... that they are forced to live at unacceptable levels of poverty' (Penrose, 2002, p 4).

To qualify for NASS payments, people seeking asylum need to show that they made their asylum claim 'as soon as reasonably practicable' after arrival in the UK. Some respondents were without support, because they did not apply at the port of entry, had not taken up the 'no choice' accommodation provided in the regions, or were in the stage of appeals. For these people informal employment was the only means of survival.

Some respondents used the window of time between when they applied for asylum and when they got a decision from the Home Office to look for informal paid work. During this time, people seeking asylum are not allowed by law to work. This wait was reported by research participants to be between one and four years. Evidence from the Refugee Council states that 'although average waiting times are reducing, some applicants are still made to wait for several months or even years for a decision on their claim' (Refugee Council, 2004, p 83). In 2003, 33% of final decisions had taken six months to process, and 13% had taken more than two years (Refugee Council, 2004). One participant, having fled from civil war, was left waiting for two years for a decision on her asylum application and started working informally:

'I have been in London for two years now; still I have no right to work because my asylum application has never been decided yet. We want to be straight, but it's as if the authorities prefer us working off the records. I don't know who gains from this situation. I could be paying my own rent, taxes and everything but now I have to take NASS vouchers and top up with cash-in-hand work. It's not my choice to work in this way, but it is imposed on me by circumstances'. (Lingala, 32)

A number of people were able to remain illegally in the UK after asylum rejection as they had found work in the informal economy. It is difficult for the government to work with people who have no legal right to remain in the country. However, intervention may be possible earlier in the process and improved efficiency of the asylum process may prevent people from entering and then becoming trapped in low-paid informal work, where they may stay even when asylum has been refused.

Foreign students

Most foreign students attending courses lasting more than six months will be given a visa that allows them to work part time during the term, up to 20 hours per week. Students interviewed said they would rather they did not have to face the 20-hour limit because they want to work and support themselves throughout their study. Given that students may have little work experience, they found that their only option was low-paid work. University of London's School of Oriental & African Studies (SOAS) posts the figure for the average student's living expenses at £930 per month. On a minimum wage, even without paying tax, 20 hours would equate to around £400 per month, leaving students with little to live on. For overseas students, the cost of studying is very high, and not all foreign students have families who can afford to support them. Others decide that the potential for improving their financial situation in the long term by gaining an education merits the risk of breaking the 20-hour barrier in the short term.

'The limitation to 20 hours for foreign students is certainly a bad thing. The cost of living here is so high. Accommodation, upkeep, books and other course-related expenses can push you into a permanent overdraft. But most students ignore the 20-hour rule and work as much as they can to make ends meet. What the restriction does is to make life difficult because you have to work in different places or take cash-in-hand work.' (Loy, 22)

While students may be aware of the 20-hour restriction before they arrive, some were not aware of the costs of living in the UK before coming here. This was also true for people who came to the UK intending to work in formal jobs.

'Recently I told my husband that we should think about going back to Lithuania. We came here thinking we would get better-paying jobs. But we can't save any money. All the money we earn goes back in bills, rent, food and taxes; so what's the point? We had jobs back home. But what we aimed for was to get better-paying jobs, save some money and invest or buy a home. I just don't think we can do it in this country, unless we do some extra cash-in-hand work that isn't taxed. (Luddimlya, 34)

Complex issues

A number of respondents described complex multiple issues in their lives, which led them to take up informal rather than formal work – issues such as debt, childcare, ill-health, lack of educational qualifications or non-recognition of those gained abroad, and immigration status. Lister (2005, p 131) points to literature that attempts to engage with the complex decisions made day to day by people living in poverty. People living in poverty are described as constantly making decisions about deployment of complex asset portfolios, for example financial, personal and social assets. For some, informal paid work is one of these assets. 'The 'traumatic' life histories of some workless 'people with multiple problems and needs' can make the most modest work ambitions difficult to achieve (Lister, 2005, p 147).

'Those with no qualifications, never had a decent job, single mothers with childcare issues, like me, those who are in debt, like me, asylum seekers who are not allowed to work or whose qualifications are not recognised, it's people in these categories. One may have one, several or all of the problems combined together. It's very difficult to get out of that situation and find formal work because so many barriers are in your way.' (Miriam, 39)

Surviving

The experience of interviewees suggests that survival rather than greed motivated their first steps into informal paid work. Poverty and child poverty are markedly high in Newham and high housing costs, low wages, high levels of people living on welfare benefits, a large number of asylum seekers and a lack of formal employment opportunities combine to fuel informal paid work.

A common theme through the interviews was that laws which try to restrict unregulated work, in an area of deprivation, go against a natural desire to survive and are bound to fail, particularly where those being targeted perceive themselves as trying to keep their children out of poverty or simply to survive.

'I really would like to work in my own name and documents, but there is no other option for me as I don't have the proper documentation that entitles me to work. It is necessity that put me in this situation and my partner is in a similar situation. But we have to continue working informally to provide a better future for our son and to look after our families at home.' (Seseko, 42, whose asylum claim was rejected after three years)

Striving

The narratives suggest that some participants wanted more than survival. Engberson (2001) distinguishes between 'life strategies' based on quality of life decisions and 'survival strategies'. Some participants wanted an income that would cover more than their basic cost of living: they wanted to be able to save for their children's education, a mortgage down-payment, healthcare, elderly relatives, extended families abroad or their own education. Some participants wanted more than a basic wage for immediate costs, for example taking holidays and buying birthday presents for their children. Even if formal work does pay enough to get by, that does not mean it will be enough to discourage informal working.

'My opinion is that some of the people who work informally do it for good reasons, and they are not necessarily all negative. In my case I was saving up money to [put a] deposit on my first home. I had a full-time job, and I was paying taxes normally. But I could not have raised deposit money in any other way, apart from borrowing, which I didn't want to do. I hate being in debt and only take absolutely necessary credit, like the mortgage.' (Sam, 43)

'There was no other way I could have realised my plans had I not done it [taken informal paid work]. At the beginning I had no right to work, but I had to save for a wedding, air ticket for my fiancée to come over here and other expenses.' (Zaramba, 34, who had fled Burundi)

Choice and restraint

It is clear that a different policy response is required for people who face hardship, to the response that is appropriate for people who work informally and can be said to be relatively wealthy. The key concern of this report is that some participants felt, for a range of reasons discussed in the previous chapter, that they had no choice but to rely on informal paid work to survive. They were constrained to informal 'opportunities', because formal opportunities were not available to them. Furthermore, people within the sample often *wanted* to move into formal paid work. It is crucial to understand why people work informally to devise effective policy. 'The shadow economy will only yield to 'inclusive' social measures that pay close attention to the motivations of people to work informally' (Jordan and Travers, 2000, p 1).

It is important for policymakers to distinguish between choice and constraint in people's actions (Burchardt and Le Grand, 2002). The next chapter looks at why informal work can provide opportunities, even if these are limited, for people who are not able to access formal work. Lister (2005), in her discussion of responses to poverty, points out that 'In the complex interplay between agency and structure, many researchers, rightly, emphasise the constraints and lack of choice faced by people in poverty and their sense of having no control over their lives' (Lister, 2005, p 132). She adds, however, that even within constraints, some decisions may be made about how to cope.

4

Sidestepping barriers to formal paid work

This chapter examines informal paid work as an alternative for participants who found it hard to access and compete in the formal job market. Respondents spoke of multiple barriers to formal work. These respondents included people arriving from overseas; young people leaving school with few qualifications; and people who had been out of work for some time or had long-term health issues. In these circumstances, participants found low-paid informal work more accessible, convenient and available. Other qualitative studies have found that entry into informal work may occur at particular life stages, such as having children, when particular barriers to formal employment occur (CESI and Boundaries Unlimited, 2006). Some participants also believed there to be discrimination by employers, whom they felt would not employ them formally due to poor health, disability, ethnicity, age, or criminal record.

Barriers to formal paid work

Participants leaving school and university perceived a lack of formal jobs matching their skills. This was cited as a major reason for taking up informal paid work. The Office of the Deputy Prime Minister acknowledges that there is 'evidence that a lack of accessible jobs is part of the problem in some places for example one third of people living in concentrations of worklessness live in a local authority with more than 10 unemployed people for every job centre vacancy. In some of these places there will be many other job opportunities that are not notified to jobcentres. In some places the informal economy offers extra opportunities which can make formal work less attractive, especially when combined with benefits' (SEU, 2004).

'I know people who finished university two years back and still have not found jobs. Government should not assume that because there is welfare, unemployed people are happy and content to sit and get benefits. If people can't find proper jobs, they will find informal work, and they will keep their benefits. Income from informal work may be helpful but it's not enough on its own to live on. Neither are benefits. How do they expect the low or no skilled to get jobs? Once this equation is solved, then government would find it easy to tackle the informal economy. It has to be recognised that people don't work informally because they like it; it's because they don't have a choice. So, the solution is providing opportunities, choice and alternatives to the informal economy.' (James, 25)

Some people felt trapped in low-paid informal work by their age, fearing no employer would employ them at this late stage in their life and felt that it would be hard to learn new skills.

'I think at 50 no one will give me a nine-to-five job and I don't want to go back to catering as I have been out of it for so long I would have to start at the bottom for low wages. I also think there is a preference for male managers in catering/hotel work. I am not well enough to go back to working more hours, I will continue to volunteer, work cash-in-hand and claim benefits, I am now a carer.' (Penelope, 50)

Respondents from overseas pointed to a lack of recognition for overseas qualifications and work experience and language barriers. Other participants suggested that skills mismatch; no or few formal qualifications; low self-esteem; and difficulty in filling in job application forms presented barriers to applying for formal work. These participants turned to low-paid informal work which offered opportunities for people with limited English language ability, limited basic skills or time constraints. This work was reported by participants to be readily available. Different participants faced different combinations of barriers, suggesting that they may benefit from tailored packages of support.

'Age, lack of UK work experience, and the fact that I have a disability have been major barriers for me to find work. I consider myself to be proficient in English and I have a degree in education, but that's not what mainstream employers think when you speak with an accent. The assumption is that you might be some ignorant African, but I taught for many years in a secondary school in Uganda. I have never worked formally in the 10 years we've lived in UK.' (Kawalya, 50, graduate teacher)

'There's this perception in the system that if your qualifications were gained abroad, then they are not good enough.... I do not think a lawyer in UK has read anything that is not covered in the law degree course in India; after all, the legal systems of Commonwealth countries were modelled on the British system. It's just a way of shutting some people out.' (Rajiv 32, lawyer, now works in the voluntary sector)

'It took me seven years to train as a doctor and by the time I left my country, I was a senior public health specialist. I have studied English but I failed one exam. I am not working as a doctor because I failed an English exam.' (Ahmed, 48, from Afghanistan)

Participants reported that some employers may not offer them a job just in case they do not have a legal right to work, even if in fact they do. While the law allows people who are legally resident to work while they are waiting for a National Insurance number, participants felt that employers do not know that they can employ people without a National Insurance number, or are unsure of the law and prefer to avoid these applicants. Follow-up interviews with a local employment agency and employers supported this view.

'When people apply and don't fill in proper information including a National Insurance number we don't invite them to interview. You don't want to end up employing 'illegals' because the fines are quite hefty if someone slipped through and they were caught.' (Herbert, runs an employment agency in Newham)

'The issue is, if you have 10 applicants to a job, you won't leave out those who have proper paperwork and go for those who don't. Not having a National Insurance number means that a person has not worked before in the UK, and has no work experience here. That's not what employers are looking for.' (Joseph, a personnel manager in Newham)

The informal and formal job search process

There are a range of reasons why people on low incomes may experience barriers to a formal job search which do not apply to an informal job search. These include the costs of the formal application process and the confidence to approach employers. The costs of looking for work in the formal sector include travel, suitable work clothes, buying newspapers, internet access, and the costs associated with writing applications, attending interviews and obtaining checks such as Criminal Records checks. For participants living on very low incomes even small costs for repeated interviews can present a major barrier to a formal job search. Informal job search through social networks mean that interviewees can avoid these costs. Research has found that 'poverty itself constitutes an obstacle to unemployed people getting jobs' (Lister, 2005, p 147). Aside from the monetary costs, Lister points to the barrier of low self confidence in finding work, stating that 'the greater the hardship, the lower the morale and self confidence are likely to be' (Lister, 2005, p 147).

Social networks

Participants spoke of obtaining informal paid work through friends or family members. Social groups, such as same-language communities or students, also pass on information about informal paid work. Networks can help people to access informal work, although only if those networks are connected to this work (Lister, 2005). Research identifies mutual trust and local understanding as a basis for informal activity, within informal networks. 'Informal recruitment operating through webs of locally based networks reduces costs to an employer' (Smith, 2005, p 154). Participants suggested that it is mutually beneficial to employer and employee to keep secret the informal nature of the work, as the employer can save on wage costs and an employee can avoid regulations.

'The people I know don't go into crime like muggings or drug dealing. They find informal work through connections and the extended family. The lucky ones get loans from their rich relatives and start their own businesses. Many others are at college, but still, most have something they do for cash, young people don't just sit there waiting for benefits, they find something to do.' (Tom, 20)

'People approach me for work, I have never had to look for work and I know many people in my local area. The sort of work available to me is cleaning, working with the 60 plus, previously working with children. This is steady permanent work. It is not easy to find cash-in-hand work, it is through contacts or approaching an employer and telling them you only want cash-in-hand work.' (Mae, 46)

Research participants reported that the formal process also required a higher level of self-confidence and proficiency in skills such as writing and presentation. The process of looking for informal work bypasses these stages, as people often access jobs through personal introduction. Research has found that those employing people in informal paid work use alternative means and standards to judge potential employees to those used in the formal recruitment situation (Smith, 2005). This means, for example, that people who may not be employed formally, such as those with a criminal record, may be taken on informally if they are known within the informal network to be reliable.

Empirical research, extending from the work of Granovetter in the 1970s, shows that people often access formal jobs through personal contact and networks rather than through the process of application, interview and selection (Ormerod and Smith, 1999).

Hannan's (1999) econometric study of routes out of unemployment reports social networks to be important. Information from these formal networks is not easily accessible to those outside of them. Research indicates that without access to the networks which lead to formal jobs, people will naturally turn to alternative networks and community groups to access informal work (Smith, 2005, p 164). In addition, distrust of government job-search agencies is also identified as a barrier to using official routes to work.

'There are not enough jobs for young people. It's hard but not impossible to find a job if you try hard. The easiest way to find a job these days is through recommendation. It's hard to get employed but once you get in, you can begin to try and get other people in.' (Moses, 24)

Availability of low-paid informal work

Participants suggested that some types of employers actively encourage informal paid work. Research suggests that governments have until recently 'conveniently ignored' the fact that certain industries encourage low-paid informal work, so that firms can compete internationally and public services can be staffed. 'Some governments have chosen to ignore parts of the informal sector in order to allow some industries or firms to compete in the international markets and to subdue protest about inadequate delivery of services' (Vasta, 2004, p 3). Participants reported that some people who do not have a legal right to work in the UK borrow or rent paperwork from contacts already living here, and present them to agencies as if they are genuine. They felt that some agencies were happy to take people with this paperwork due to critical staff shortages in some areas, such as care work. However, some participants reported that agencies were becoming increasingly strict with paperwork.

'I have been doing care work with an agency, I was earning £100 per week, but I lost the job two months ago. I was asked for a CRB [Criminal Records Bureau] certificate which I don't have. I registered with the agency using a friend's identity papers but she did not give me a CRB. Agencies are getting very strict, even when you have been working with them for long, when they ask for CRB you have to produce it, if you happen to be in a situation like mine, using another person's papers, you just leave quietly.' (Milly, 29)

Discussion with focus group members (policymakers and practitioners) indicates that in certain industries informal working is particularly widespread, such as construction and cleaning services. In such industries contractors put a distance between the main employer and the informal worker, and complex tiers of subcontractors make the industry hard to regulate (Smith, 2005). This means that large reputable establishments, such as supermarkets and local authorities, may indirectly pay for informal work, with low wages and poor conditions. An increasing trend towards subcontracted employment in the low-paid economy has been identified (Evans et al, 2005). This suggests that in pursuit of efficiency, through contracting out work, the options for informal paid work are increasing and, possibly, that these informal jobs replace work that was once undertaken by formally employed staff.

Small local businesses also need low-paid workers to survive. 'For the small employer, cash workers represent the ultimate flexible labour force, allowing them to adjust their demand for labour as business conditions dictate' (Smith, 2005, p 152). It is likely that if this kind of low-paid work was taxed, it would not be worthwhile for the employee financially to undertake the work. Smith goes on to point out that 'it is these sectors (micro-business) that local authorities enthusiastically endorse in their economic regeneration strategies, while condemning the 'informal economy' and criminalising its workforce' (Smith, 2005, p 153).

We have eight full-time staff. They do hair, manicure and pedicure, sun bed and two men's barbers. I work there myself – weekends and holidays and my mum pays me as casual staff. She has about 10 casual workers who come in as and when needed. If we are busy or have taken more than usual bookings, she will call them in. They are sort of a back-up so that we don't lose customers. My mum said they are self-employed people, so they are supposed to make arrangements for themselves as far as taxes are concerned. Well, we are all supposed to be responsible for our actions really. We can't police casual workers like that; otherwise you end up with no one willing to work, and if you are a small business – that affects you. It's up to them what they do with their money.' (Sally, 19)

Focus group participants reported that in some industries, employers use the strategy of saying that employees are self-employed. In this way, the responsibility for declaring and paying taxes is passed to the employee, and the employer can pay at a level below the national minimum wage (NMW). This activity has been included as informal paid work, for the purpose of this report. This is also found in other research. 'The introduction of the NMW and employment legislation is likely to accelerate the trend towards self-employment as firms attempt to gain a competitive advantage and absolve themselves from any obligation to the worker' (Smith, 2005, p 153). One participant reported that he could only get a wage below the NMW in a local construction firm as other people were working as self-employed, on Construction Industry Scheme (CIS) cards. Other studies indicate that this pattern goes beyond London (CESI and Boundaries Unlimited, 2006).

Participants spoke of a blurred line between employees and volunteers, with organisations wanting to pay volunteers for their work when they could afford to. This had to be informal so that people could carry on claiming benefits since the organisation could not consistently afford to pay them enough to live on.

'I have come across informal work arrangements both at work and at home. In my previous job, which was also in the voluntary sector, quite often there was a blurred boundary between volunteering and paid work. At times some of our volunteers would receive some payment for a bit of extra work or would be asked to stand in for a sick or absent employee for a day or two to cover reception or a bit of admin work. We would pay them cash-in-hand using petty cash. And these were mostly people we knew, maybe a friend's daughter, a lone parent known to be in need or a removals van man known to a member of staff would be asked to do a delivery job if we bought some new furniture or office equipment. Such transactions were paid for from our petty cash.' (Laura, 31)

Attraction of informal work

Informal work was seen by participants to be more flexible than formal work. One young person described this as having a sense of being your own boss. Smith (2005) identifies a feeling of freedom that is attached to informal work and states that informal work 'gives the freedom to leave jobs that are often too menial to perform for sustained periods of time' (p 157). Other qualitative research identifies flexibility as a key factor in the decision to take up formal work (CESI and Boundaries Unlimited, 2006).

'It's also flexible, you are not tied to any sort of contracts and can quit whenever you want and can come back to the same job if you are in need of money again.' (Gilbert, 20)

I think the informal arrangements are very flexible. For example if you get stuck with the kids and you can't do a shift, you can ask a friend to do it. All they care about is that the job is done, not who has done it. If you fail to get a friend to cover you, they will still understand. You don't get the sack like in a normal job because they understand your situation. I am only talking about my situation and those people that I know. I don't know what happens with other people working informally. Maybe it's not flexible everywhere. You get paid less but it is the flexibility that is very appealing.' (Janet, 34)

A number of parents spoke of taking up low-paid informal work to fit around new childcare responsibilities. They could not find formal employment with hours that were flexible enough to fit around the childcare that was available to them. They could find informal work that was in shifts or short slots that they could work around their childcare needs. Focus group participants pointed to the complex logistics of taking children of different ages to different nurseries and schools, at different times.

'Night work suits me because day time I have to be there for the children. Drop them off to school, pick them up later, do their washing, meals. Looking after three children is a full-time job in itself. Benefits money cannot even take me through three days with the kids, we would have to miss meals if I was relying on Income Support alone.... Whenever I think about working formally, I ask myself, what job could give me enough for rent, childcare, Council Tax, pay my bills and leave enough for me and the kids to feed on?' (Butera, 38, single father with three children, drives a van delivering newspapers at night)

Over the longer term, having been in low-paid informal work, these participants found themselves excluded from the formal job market, lacking the confidence or up-to-date skills to return to formal work. While they would have liked to work formally, they were not able to. Some respondents also found childcare a barrier to informal work. However, one participant pointed out that her job was easy to return to again once she had resolved the childcare issue.

Some people were able to save on childcare costs because they could take their children with them in some cases of informal work, for example in childcare and domestic work, tailoring work from home and staffing local launderettes. Informal work also provided a way of keeping in touch with the world of work, when people felt too vulnerable to take on a regular formal job outside of the home, and didn't feel able to declare their work in case they lost their benefits.

'I earn a bit of cash working at my mother's launderette. I help out during the week and get £80 in cash for 20 hours a week. It fits in well with my life because I take my baby with me; it would be boring sitting at home all day, plus I earn a bit of money which helps me with the bills. But it's a good way of keeping a foot in the world of work; otherwise you can eventually become work shy if you sit and do nothing at all for years. I would rather I did something than nothing at all.' (Kim, 22, has a 10-month-old baby)

The employer–employee relationship

Research has found that some employer–employee relationships in the informal sector 'are based more on co-operation than domination' (Williams and Windebank, 2004a, p 5). The current study also finds that some informal workers and those who employ them have a cordial mutual relationship. The employer is aware that the worker claims benefits, or has no right to work, but still employs as a way of helping. But the employer gains too, because the average wage paid in these circumstances is the minimum wage or below. This suggests that a relationship with an informal employer may be at once exploitative and supportive. Most of the informal work that the people in our sample engaged in was low-paid and routine, rather than well-paid, autonomous and non-routine. However, people in these situations spoke of support and assistance from their employers in making the transition to formal employment, such as providing work experience and references.

Follow-up interviews with informal employers suggest that they have some sympathy for people who are in need and who are working and claiming benefits, and in particular for people who need to be flexible due to their childcare needs. They deliberately 'turn a blind eye' because they understand that there is little alternative for these people. This finding echoes that in the estate-based research of Smith (2005), where a case is discussed in which a subcontracted gardener is employing young people excluded from formal work due to low skills and convictions: 'While he would seem to be exploiting his workforce through paying them less than he would be obliged to under NMW legislation, the employer also insists that he is motivated by altruistic concerns' (Smith, 2005, p 150).

'We have two young single-parent female staff I know who are on benefits but we give them cash work. They both take home £100 each per week if they cover their shifts. They can only do flexible shifts and sometimes they don't turn up because of kids trouble. In their circumstances you can tell they would not manage with a mainstream full-time job. Only if you are local and understand local issues would you be sympathetic to just help out.' (Fazlur, 34, manager)

Informal employers were seen by research participants as helping those who needed to earn some extra cash and cannot find formal work. As has been found in other studies (Williams and Windebank, 1998), informal employment was frequently a vehicle for family members to support individuals in time of need without an implication of giving charity. Research indicates that some informal paid work takes place in 'a kind of moral economy' of private households and neighbourhoods and is more based on solidarity and help in social networks' (Pfau-Effinger, 2003, cited in Vasta et al, 2004, p 8).

'I couldn't use my benefits to pay my debts, as that was my kid's lifeline and I owed a lot. But a good Samaritan who is my former manager at the betting shop – offered me part-time cash evening work.' (Jane, 40)

Exploitation of people who arrive in a country from abroad by others from their country has been noted (Tilly, 1990; Jordan and Duvell, 2002). Participants felt that not all employers were helpful. Some were exploitative, requiring them to work long shifts and offering little pay.

'I had a bad experience as an informal employee in a garage. I was paid less than the minimum wage, worked long hours and got the sack when I took a week off work due to my son's illness. The most frustrating thing was that I could not complain anywhere because I was on benefits.' (Chris, 38)

Benefits of informal paid work

While employers can be exploitative, there are benefits to the existence of informal paid work that could be harnessed. Informal employers enabled people who faced barriers to formal work to access employment. They also helped people to find temporary solutions to crises. Participants' stories identify a range of benefits, other than income, including increased confidence, skills and work experience, and potential pathways into formal work. There are also potentially family, community and social benefits from informal work, including increased social cohesion (Pfau-Effinger, 2003).

People in low-paid informal work are in themselves a potential resource to the economy as a whole. Suggestions for realising this potential can be found in Chapter 9. These people want to work and have skills and abilities, often above those that the work they are doing demands. They may also be resourceful and resilient through managing the stresses of living on a low income.

The Office of the Deputy Prime Minister points to evidence that there is hidden potential within the informal economy. It cites the fact that voluntary and commercial agencies like At Work and Street UK see a number of clients currently working or trading illegally who want to find regular jobs or legalise their businesses as identifying this potential. They also state that 'in some concentrations of worklessness, there is, in fact, a great deal of 'work' going on, and evidence of considerable entrepreneurial spirit and skills which could potentially be harnessed for the formal economy'(SEU, 2004, p 46).

5

Informal work as a response to crisis

This chapter looks at participants facing crisis points in their lives who turn to informal paid work due to the urgency of their need to find income, such as after a redundancy or marital breakdown. Some have incurred debt and turn to informal paid work to service and repay the debt. At this crisis point, the time that it would take to find a formal job makes informal work a more rational option.

Financial crisis

Many people in the UK risk sudden financial crisis. Oxfam states that over 10.5 million people live in financial insecurity. 'They can't afford to save, insure their house contents, or spend even small amounts on themselves. About 9.5 million can't afford adequate housing – heated, free from damp, and in a decent state of decoration. The crucial factor about these findings is that they are based on a survey of what the general population sees as necessities' (BOND et al, 2005).

Participants reported that debt was a factor pushing them into informal work. Some participants were working informally as a way of servicing debts without losing benefits, or to top up their income. Research has found that people on low wages or benefits may regularly experience some form of debt. 'Low-income households frequently fall behind with their basic household bills such as rent, mortgage, gas, electricity, water and council tax. Most people feel ashamed of their debts, but their situation is one of 'can't pay' rather than 'won't pay' (Kempson, 1996).

£49 billion is owed by UK credit card customers. In 2004, 6.1 million families had difficulties in meeting their debt repayments (Financial Services Authority, 2003). Some individuals manage to secure reduced repayment rates for loans when they are on low incomes. This may encourage people to remain on benefits, and to work informally rather than formally, for fear of the higher repayment rates being reinstated.

Many people in deprived areas live day to day, and are unable to make decisions on a long-term basis (Lister, 2005). In this context, the relative risks of working informally are assessed in a short-term framework. People will risk taking informal work in order to avert more immediate situations such as going hungry or being threatened by debt collectors. Some participants were aware that they are doing something that is illegal, while others were not. For some participants who were aware, however, a decision was made between taking what were perceived as immediate and more distant risks. Being caught for fraud seemed a more distant and less threatening prospect than the immediate risk of destitution or debt collectors.

> 'It haunts me to realise that I am committing benefit fraud, but I suppose I had no choice because being in debt is not the better option; at least I paid off most of my debt; otherwise bailiffs could have been on my door.' (Kaylie, 37, lone parent)

Fear of debt

Some people feared that loss of benefits on taking up formal employment would leave them in financial crisis. Community Links advice staff have reported that debt is often linked to returning to work from being on benefits. For those participants who did not already have debts, informal work was a response to the fear that having to live on such a low income may lead to debt, if benefits such as Housing Benefit were lost. Some also feared that delays in run-on benefit payments, or reinstated payment, if they were to lose their job, would lead them to build up arrears.

Family breakdown

Several participants had turned to informal paid work at a time of family crisis, such as divorce. Family breakdown can be a time of sudden loss of income and create an urgent need to fill this gap. Smith (2005, p 156) finds in his estate-based study of informal activity that 'a reassessment of available economic opportunities often occurred during a period of transition in the respondent's lifecycles'. He found that a time of change such as this could lead to a readjustment in expectations, status and lifestyle.

For some participants this was also a time of additional difficulties such as homelessness, which may make it even more difficult to find formal work, due to stress and disruption, and the high rents charged for temporary accommodation. One participant, for example, was an experienced mechanic in Pakistan but when he came to the UK with his British wife, things did not turn out the way he had expected. He separated from his wife and found himself homeless and eventually in temporary accommodation. The high costs of temporary accommodation meant that if he had taken up formal work, he would have had to live in poverty, as he would have to pay most of his salary in rent, therefore he would be better off staying on benefits.

Job search in times of crisis

Finding informal paid work can be much easier and faster than finding formal employment. For those in crisis, it feels reasonable to take the first opportunity to change the situation. For example, one mother on benefits suddenly incurred large debts when her business start-up failed. She did not have time to go through formal job search processes before paying creditors. She opted for informal paid work, which was readily available. Aside from institutional and personal barriers to formal paid work, some reasons for participants entering low-paid informal work can be explained by their attitudes, towards society, their circumstances and work. The next chapter sets out a typology of four different attitudes towards low-paid informal work that can be identified from the interviews.

6

Attitudes to low-paid informal work: towards a typology

This chapter looks at respondents' attitudes and how these impact on their decision to work informally. Lister's (2005) research into poverty in the UK suggests a typology of reactions to poverty. This includes four categories: 'getting by', 'getting back at', 'getting out' and 'getting organised'. That is, people who struggle to get by every day; those who use strategies of everyday resistance; those who use strategies to get out of poverty; and those who get together to effect wider change. A similar typology begins to emerge from the attitudes of the interviewees towards low-paid informal work. This chapter sets out a brief summary of each type of reaction. There are those participants who were unaware of the law; those for whom informal working is a family or social norm; those who realise that they are doing wrong; others who justify their informal work; and those who turn a blind eye.

Unaware of the law

Some participants worked in low-paid informal work and were not aware that they are required to pay tax on cash income and that they may be breaking the law by taking and not declaring cash payment. Some people knew in theory of the benefits of formal working, but have never experienced them and saw them as beyond their reach. Some participants stated that they did not know what would happen to them if they were caught working cash-in-hand.

> 'I thought it was another form of working and getting paid in cash, because I don't even have a bank account and where I work is a family business. All the three workers in the warehouse get paid in cash.' (Tarek 21)

There was a particular lack of awareness among young people that informal paid work was illegal, or different in any way from formal work. Participants assumed that cash went through the books as any other pay. For other young people, the decision to work informally was not rational, rather it was impulsive: they wanted a job, they did not necessarily think through the implications, but just took the first thing that they were offered

> 'I think cash-in-hand jobs aren't reliable, it should be a second job, or something you do while looking for a permanent job. Before this interview I had no idea that it was illegal to do cash-in-hand work. I thought it was just another way to get paid. Some employees with no bank accounts chose to get paid in cash because that's the only way they can be paid anyway.' (Muktar,17)

'My peers don't see the informal paid work as a problem. In fact, I would say 90% of my peers don't even know what the informal economy means, all they care about is: are there opportunities out there to make some quick bucks? Then they go for them.' (Cliff, 19)

Informal paid work as a norm

Some participants wanted to stop working informally, fearing being caught, or wanted a better, formal job so that they could advance in life. These people faced a range of barriers to formal work, as discussed in the previous chapters. Other research participants learned to live with informal working as a norm, and for a number it was seen as acceptable, even desirable by the family. For some there was a sense that everyone else is doing it, which sanctioned their own actions. Other respondents said that cash-in-hand work was their first and only experience of work. Smith (2005, p 157) finds that 'the tactics and knowledge that allow individuals to circumvent formal institutions and to construct lives either outside of, or on the margins of formal employment, are based in a generational consciousness among those who have known little else'.

'I know many people working cash-in-hand as builders, caterers, giving tuition to kids, doing domestic cleaning and childcare ... informal working is so widespread that people regard it as another way of working and earning a living.' (Naila, 32, tailors garments at home for sale)

'I have no experience whatsoever of working formally, I can say I have no reason to encourage people to do formal work, because I haven't got a clue what it is about myself. I am aware that I miss out on things like holiday pay, pension schemes and credit facilities, but I don't see how I can change my situation now.' (Jan, 40, left school with few qualifications, worked informally in a number of jobs and now has a more stable informal job on a market stall earning £180 per week)

'People round here just see it as work; most people don't see it as breaking the law. They just see it as another way to make ends meet. The East End of London works like that, it has been renowned for ducking and diving and hustling over the years, and for some people here, that is a way of life.' (John, 49)

Aware of the law, but preferring to work

Some respondents did not consider benefits an option, preferring to do low-paid informal work rather than claim benefits. For some this was a matter of self-respect and fear of the stigma of signing on for benefits. Research suggests that the work ethic remains, and some people therefore chose informal work over benefit (Smith, 2005, p 190).

'The cash-in-hand work meant that I did not need to claim benefits for the six months I was unemployed because I could support myself. I just couldn't face joining a dole queue. There's stigma attached to claiming benefits and I couldn't afford to be seen standing in a dole queue every week or whatever.' (Martin, 32)

Some respondents preferred to avoid the benefits system altogether due to what they described as the hostile environment encountered on trying to claim. That is, they felt that staff had been unhelpful and found the system difficult to understand.

'Most people I know from my community treat benefits offices as unwelcoming places. No one would report to benefits people – even if they knew someone works informally and claims benefit. There's a permanent mutual suspicion and mistrust between claimants and officials. The two don't trust each other.' (Kingston, 29)

Mike is a young man living from hand to mouth, but could not claim Jobseeker's Allowance, as he described himself as a proud young man who would rather work at something than sign on and do nothing. Undeclared work in response to poverty can be a way of maintaining autonomy and dignity.

'I am a 20-year-old black male living in Canning Town with my 60-year-old mother. I am currently unemployed and I haven't had a steady job for over a year. I used to work as a bouncer at a nightclub. I found the job very stressful as the hours were unsocial. I am entitled to Jobseeker's Allowance, but I don't claim it. As a proud stubborn young black man, the dole queue is not for me. I would rather work off the books for now and if I find a better formal job, I'll take it, but meanwhile am self-sufficient.' (Mike, 20)

Aware of the law, but justifying informal work

Participants identified a type of person who justified their informal work. A recent qualitative research study of people in informal activity in Merseyside (CESI and Boundaries Unlimited, 2006) also finds the existence of a work ethic, of people who justify their informal work – whether or not on a low income – who had considered their actions and were aware of the effect they would have on others. The justifications illustrated by the quotes below include a reaction against perceptions of unfair tax and benefits systems and need. There was a sense of informal paid work providing a kind of social justice. Lister (2005) points out 'unreported work, within the limits set by need rather than greed, can take on a certain legitimacy and is often condoned in deprived areas' (Lister, 2005, p 139).

'I think the main motivation behind young people working informally is that they don't like taxes being subtracted from their small wages. This means that if you do cash-in-hand work, you get more money. Why would you want to work hard, and not get the money you deserve? When the pay cheque comes and you see how much tax was taken, it hurts. The first thought that comes to mind is, why this much?' (David, 20)

'The government is greedy. Why would they want to tax someone earning £150 a week? I don't think I have to volunteer to pay taxes on my £150. We are struggling as it is. Rent alone for the two-bedroom house we live in is £800 per month. Fortunately, my boyfriend pays the rent because he's in a good job. Me, I take cash-in-hand work by looking after kids and I work from home.' (Khadija, 30)

'I've never met anyone who is really disturbed by it [cash-in-hand work]. Most people round here don't care. They know it's against the law, but so are a lot of things ... like dropping litter. I think that most people round here see it in that context and for many it is unavoidable. In this area it's the done thing.' (Phillip, 58)

'But our needs as a family were way beyond the benefits I was getting. So my informal work was basically sort of a coping mechanism. I needed some extra cash, I went out when I could, I earned it; I did not steal the money, that's how many people feel when they are working in this way. If the government can solve the problem around childcare, many parents in my situation would be working.' (Sarah, 46)

'In my view, informal working is common and generally accepted as a way of earning a living. It is not something we think of as crime, despite all this government publicity about benefit fraud. There are so many people who are entitled to benefits but don't claim, either because they don't know they are entitled, or because they find the system complicated and impenetrable. I think the situation cancels itself out. People don't believe government loses a lot of money in benefit fraud because it could be argued that similar amounts go unclaimed by those entitled but unaware or unable to claim for one reason or another.' (Jo, 27)

Some participants also felt that the work they did informally had social value. Some people interviewed felt they contributed to the economy in their own way, by caring for others in the family. They felt entitled to earn a little over their benefits in reward. Some people do not see avoiding paying taxes as shameful, whereas they do see claiming benefits as shameful. They see their informal work as keeping them off benefits where they cannot find a regular job.

'The government must understand that immigrants do all the jobs that people here don't want to do, so they are not useless and they contribute enormously to the economy.' (Kagezi, 30, hospital porter, works on 'borrowed papers' waiting for asylum)

'The mothers of the kids I look after are my friends. This is an arrangement between me and them. If I registered I would have to declare my earnings, pay taxes and lose benefits. I don't want to do that until I am in a secure job. Plus, I am helping others to go to work by looking after the children; so it's not bad.' (Keeza, 29)

'I feel I pay back my social security benefits by helping others. I do a lot of voluntary work. People that work nine to five cannot do voluntary work, so it falls onto someone like myself. If you put together the efforts of those who volunteer, the work they do pays for their benefits.' (Laura, 24)

'Turning a blind eye'

Some people interviewed felt that 'turning a blind eye' would be the best strategy for dealing with people in low-paid informal work. They felt that people should not be punished, and that they should be allowed to work informally to make ends meet.

'To be quite honest I don't really care about the informal paid work because it sustains a lot of people. I wonder how such people would survive if there was no such work. In the Asian communities people do a lot of cash-in-hand work, employ family members, relatives, but it is seen as helping others, not cheating the government. Government itself wastes taxpayers' money on useless things like the Dome, so there isn't that much sympathy for the taxman. People will try if they can to avoid paying taxes.' (Rajiv, 32)

7

Experiences of low-paid informal work: case studies

The case studies and viewpoints presented in this chapter illustrate some of the many different situations that have led people to work informally. The case studies demonstrate the need for a diversity of responses to the issues of low-paid informal work. All names have been changed to retain confidentiality.

Case Study One: Rasheed

Surviving: a parent's benefits trap

Rasheed carries out a mix of formal and informal work so as to keep some benefits. As the carer of a disabled child called Amina, Rasheed's wife cannot work. He has to find additional money to afford the costs of Amina's care. The main reason why Rasheed feels he cannot declare his work to the benefits agency is that he would not be able to afford to pay rent and Council Tax if these were not covered by benefits.

'I am married with one child and I work as a cleaner. I have lived and worked in Newham for eight years. My daughter is disabled, so my wife can't go to work because she has to care for her full-time.

I declare less hours of work to the benefits office, as I would not be eligible for some of the benefits that I get if I declared fully. I earn £100 per week and this is what I declare. This means that I am still entitled to Housing Benefit and Council Tax Benefit. But even then, with the extra care needs of my daughter given that my wife doesn't work, I have to do something.

I do some cleaning work and I don't declare this as it's paid cash-in-hand. It's mostly people I know, local businesses and homes. This gives me an extra £150 per week and I have been doing this for four years now. I worry about this situation in case I get caught but I feel I have no alternative but to do it. To be able to look after my family and take care of their needs – I have to continue working in this way unless I win the Lottery.

I get paid £6 per hour in my formal employment. But when I do the same job for cash-in-hand, I get paid £4 per hour but it's cash, no tax. That's why there is a permanent demand for informal workers; you will find work if you have good contacts. In Newham it's easy to find work informally.

Poverty makes people work informally because they are struggling to make ends meet. If you are in extreme need you won't think twice about taking cash-in-hand work. You can't tell needy people to stop working informally because that is the way they survive and look after their families; you have to provide an alternative in order to stop this.

The minimum wage should be increased to £8 per hour at least. I also think that people on low pay should be allowed to keep some of their benefits especially Housing Benefit or should not be taxed. Most of the people I know say that they could do without other benefits but not Housing Benefit because rents are high in this area.'

Case Study Two: Joe

Striving: managing to study

Jo saw informal work as the only way to study; partly because of the low benefits levels and partly for fear of delays in the benefits system leaving Joe in financial difficulty. Joe did not want to get into debt.

'I managed to go through university because I had an informal temping job. On benefits alone, it would have been next to impossible. Benefits levels are very low. Sometimes you wonder if those who set the rates for benefits ever tried living on them. They are awfully inadequate. I worked informally throughout the time I spent at university and it was a matter of keeping my head above the water rather than cheating the system. I had to take care of the needs of my children in the best way I could, which in this case was carrying on with temping work, but not declaring it.

The second problem is the administrative nightmare of a service the benefit offices provide. When I started the temping job, I initially informed my local benefits office and coped well on reduced benefit because it was a part-time job. But when I stopped working, they kept me on reduced benefits as if I was in work, despite the fact that I had notified them. It took weeks of telephone calls, visits and letters to rectify that problem. I decided after that incident, I wasn't going to put myself and the kids in that situation again. When I got some more temping work, I never told them about it and for two years I had this £150 bi-weekly income from a temping agency. I was paid by cheque but I never gave my national insurance number.'

Case Study Three: Naomi

Barriers to work: working around childcare needs

For Naomi, childcare presents a major barrier to formal working where jobs tend to be inflexible. In addition, she has difficulty in making the transition from being a full-time mother into paid employment outside of the home. Naomi wants to return to work, but struggles with the uncertainty of whether her training course will run to completion.

'It has been very difficult for me to find work because of the long period I have spent out of work. I looked after my children when they were younger and it is now difficult to get into formal employment. I lack experience and confidence because I have not worked formally for 18 years and don't have any new technology skills, for example using a computer.

I am better off on benefits for now. As a full-time mother I wanted to care well for my children and when you are single, children are more demanding. Now that my children are older I am able to study and when I finish my course I will look for a job.

I have been doing cash-in-hand work as a hairdresser cutting and colouring hair for about six years. I work from home. When my husband left I could not manage and the children were young. I claimed benefits but did not have enough money to live on. I never talk about being on benefits as I am embarrassed and I think I would lose my benefits if I declared my small income from hairdressing. My customers have a low income and it helps them to come to me as my charges are much lower than in the salons.

[To help them to get into a full-time job] people should have training that is good quality and then get good wages. More advice about making the change from working informally to formally, how will this affect my benefits, will I be able to manage? When you haven't worked for so long it is a big step to go back into formal working and I think there should be more support than available currently.

The benefits are not sufficient and the unmet needs force people to look for alternatives. Flexible working would help women bringing up children. Government should support voluntary and community groups to improve the lives of people living on benefits.'

Case Study Four: Saira

Barriers to work: working around health needs

Saira faces multiple issues. She has just received the right to work after four years waiting for her asylum claim to be processed. She is a lone parent with a medical condition, and does not see formal work as an option due to her health needs.

'Until about eight months ago, I had no right to work in this country although I have lived here for four years. My asylum application had never been decided. I only got leave to remain recently.

The money I get in benefits is not enough for me to live on with my son. If I told them about what I earn cash-in-hand, my benefits would be stopped. Some people out there think because you get these benefits you are comfortable; which is not the case. I still struggle to pay my bills. Finding informal work is a struggle for survival. You have to think of ways to get by. The needs are even greater if you have children. I know for a fact that the percentage paid for childcare by government doesn't go far enough. It would not entice me to go into formal work.

The women whose kids I look after are working informally too. One is a hairdresser and the other works as a cleaner, but they can't claim Child Tax Credits because I am not registered. I know that they earn about £150 each because we discussed all these issues before I agreed to look after the kids. There are people who can't do without benefits and the reason for working informally is to top up. There are those who don't even have the benefits either because they aren't entitled, or their residence status does not allow them to claim, so they struggle to survive in the informal economy.

I started working informally because of the long wait for papers from the Home Office. Should I have spent four years sitting and waiting? Also I can't be sure that if I took a formal job, an employer would put up with my frequent hospital visits or absence from work. I have a medical condition that means that I have to attend hospital check-ups monthly and sometimes I get unwell because of the medicines I take.

At times I feel well enough to work, but if I got a regular job and then became unwell, it is very difficult to regain benefits, so I decide to keep benefits and work off the books – if and when I can. My son and I have needs that are beyond the benefits we get. I look after children for a bit of cash and that helps us. Most parents can't afford registered childminders who charge twice or more of my rate. People use us because we are cheaper, plus they trust us. It's easier to let a friend or neighbour look after your child than a total stranger, don't you think so?'

Case Study Five: Jane

A time of crisis: debts

Jane, a lone parent of four children, was heavily indebted to illegal lenders – 'loan sharks'. Jane was on benefits and had tried to set up her own business without success. At the same time her partner left her and she had to pay the money she owed alone. She was offered informal paid work which she could start straight away to help her sort out her debt problem. If she declared her earnings she would lose benefit and not be able to support her family. If she had waited to find a formal job she would have faced confrontation with the 'loan sharks'.

'I am a single mother of four, the youngest is six, and the eldest is 19 – just started university. I have been out of work for five years now. I have done various jobs in the past – care assistant, betting shop attendant and waitress. I left school at 16 with no qualifications.

In the last two years I have been working for cash-in-hand. I do four evenings a week at a local betting shop. I ran into debt problems and the only way out was to find some way of earning some money to pay back. I couldn't use my benefits to pay debts, as that's my family's lifeline, and I owed a lot. But a good samaritan who was my former manager offered me this cash-in-hand job.

I work four hours Tuesday to Friday. I get paid £100 cash on Friday evenings. I know what I am doing may be benefit fraud, but I had no choice. I was being threatened by the people I owed money to and had to do something about the situation before it got out of hand. My family was being threatened if I didn't pay up.

I borrowed money for urgent problems, but the lenders were loan sharks, it was not a bank. I suspect they are money launderers because they pass themselves off as a business, but they have no physical address. The way they deal with their customers it looks dodgy. When you fail with repayments, they send some big guys round your house to threaten you.'

Case Study Six: Margaret

Informal working as a norm

Margaret has never worked formally. At the age of 50, for her it is a way of life. She does not describe herself as socially excluded, or exploited, just that informal work was the type of work that was available to her. Margaret describes informal working as a social norm. Margaret also points to the increasing expense of keeping children happy as a driver towards informal work. Other studies indicate that pressures on families with children to spend money are increasing (Ridge, 2005).

'I trained as a dancer. I worked as a dancer for five to six years until I was 34. I found the work through agencies and contacts. I enjoyed the work, I had a good social life and made good friends. The pay was very good. The work fitted in with my childcare responsibilities. I would get my money there and then after dancing. I have done bar work on and off since I was 19 up until I was 50. I was earning at the beginning £3.50 per hour, when I stopped I was earning £6 per hour. I got the jobs through word of mouth and was paid cash weekly. I liked the dancing job because I could fit it around the children. In the evening my mum would look after the children and I would go to work.

The government could encourage bigger business to provide childcare and give government money to smaller businesses to provide childcare. This would encourage lots of women back to work. There should be more childcare provision for parents who want to go to college or university.

I think there is a lot of informal work going on, people have done work for me and I have paid cash-in-hand, I have friends who work cash-in-hand. The type of cash-in-hand work going on is delivering newspapers, advertising leaflets and minicab cards, catering, building work, labouring, painting and decorating, childminding, car mechanics, panel beaters, tree cutting, the list is endless. Working informally has a mutual benefit, you pay less for the job and the employee pays no tax. I am one person who has never done a job on the books all my life.

People work cash-in-hand because they live outside their means. Benefits are very basic and are difficult to live on. Society is very materialistic. When I was young my father made me a dolls' house which I thought was amazing. Now if a child wants a dolls house it costs £200. Children have peer pressure for designer labels; you don't want your child to be bullied for not wearing the right stuff.

Some employers prefer to pay cash-in-hand as it is easier and cheaper, particularly small businesses or community organisations with a small budget.'

8

Overview of current policy

This chapter examines current government policy on low-paid informal work, and the relevance of this policy for people facing poverty, crisis and barriers to formal employment. The issue of informal low-paid work cuts across government agendas: Tax Credits and welfare to work, welfare benefits reform, anti-poverty, regeneration, community cohesion, financial inclusion, health, immigration and education. This is not intended as an exhaustive overview. Rather, it covers key issues arising directly in relation to the research undertaken.

Supportive, not punitive, policy

Over the last five years there has been increased activity, interest and recognition around the issues of the informal economy from individual government departments, particularly Revenue & Customs, the Treasury and the Department of Trade and Industry. A cross-government working group exists to look at the national agenda. However, existing policies are eclectic and contradictory, and there remains no clear cross-government strategy with a view to helping those in informal low-paid work make the transition to formal employment.

The Office of the Deputy Prime Minister acknowledges the existence of informal paid work among those with a low income, in some areas of 'worklessness', in its report *Jobs and enterprise in deprived areas* (SEU, 2004, p 9). It states that 'the Government will do more to ensure that measures like in-work Tax Credit reach the people they are intended to help. The freedoms open to local managers and advisers in Jobcentre Plus should allow them to do more to address clients' concerns about the impact of returning to work'. However, it has yet to implement a stream of work or develop policies that include the issue of the informal economy.

Tax Credits

Revenue & Customs have not yet made public their strategies for supporting people who wish to leave informal paid work. However, the Tax Credit system is a measure that could potentially pull people from informal to formal paid work. In-work benefits and other welfare-to-work measures have had some success in getting people from welfare to work (Parliamentary Ombudsman Report, 2005). However, not all people are reached by these measures (Griggs et al, 2005).

Child Tax Credits and Working Tax Credits were introduced in 2003 to provide financial support for families and people on low incomes. Under this system, means-tested support for parents and children is separated. Adults can claim Jobseeker's Allowance, Income Support or Tax Credits, for themselves, and Child Tax Credit for their children. For a family with a child, to claim Working Tax Credit one or both parents must work over 16 hours per week. In order to qualify, at least one partner must work over 30 hours in a week. Policymakers and service providers who participated in the study felt that this could exclude people who are on low incomes but may not be able to find work of over 16 hours or 30 hours per week.

One research participant who is a mother of two children takes her baby to domestic cleaning in between a school run. She says she earns £100 per week cash-in-hand but sometimes gets no work at all.

Childcare element

The Tax Credits system creates a disincentive for a second earner in a family to work formally. If a second earner worked full time, then the family would be no better off, and therefore they may be encouraged to remain as the childcarer and to work informally. For example, a family with one earner on just above the minimum wage, at £11,000 per year, would take home just over £130 a week. If that family had one baby, and the second partner returned to work full time, then, based on childcare of £175 per week, the family would have a disposable income of around £95 per week, including Tax Credits, and not get to spend time with the children. This figure does not take into account additional payments for rent, council tax, travel and other in-work expenses, and debt repayments.

'Government only pays a percentage of childcare costs and expect me to find the rest; from where? It wouldn't make any difference in my financial situation now getting a job. Remember, if I started working now, I would have to pay rent, which is £700 a month. I would have to pay Council Tax, which is £100 per month. When you add childcare costs, and the bills, it makes no sense on the kind of wage I am capable of earning. It's better for me to stay on benefits and see what I can do on the side.' (Nadia, 26)

Few interviewees recognised Tax Credits as something that may encourage people to work formally. It was clear that many people were not aware that they might be eligible for Tax Credits. In 2003/04, one in five people entitled to Tax Credits did not claim (CPAG, 2005). Non-take-up of benefits is widely reported (CAB, 2003). Respondents in this research sample had not made use of this support. Some had entered informal work before the introduction of Tax Credits and for a range of reasons, for example, lack of confidence or a lack of up-to-date work experience, found themselves unable to find formal work and take advantage of Tax Credits. All the barriers to formal work, detailed in previous chapters, render the incentive of Tax Credits ineffective. Steep overpayment recovery rates have left some claimants with negative Tax Credit payable; in one case at Community Links, overpayment was £6,000 but the Tax Credit award for the next year was £3,000. Some respondents knew of Tax Credits, but did not believe that they would be better off if they applied for them.

'If you are on benefits and considering going back to work, with all the insecurities as well as a family to look after, this is not a situation you want to walk into and you have to know that locally, if one family gets these problems, many others will know and soon the message is that 'don't even bother, Tax Credits are a mess'. (Advice worker)

Research participants also reported that people were confused or afraid of applying for Tax Credits. Community Links advice workers report the Tax Credits system to be extremely complicated to calculate. In all, Working Tax Credit is made up of seven elements. Furthermore, advice staff felt that individuals would find it hard to understand the significance of a yearly lump sum, when they live on a week-by-week basis. At one of the focus groups in this study into perceptions of the benefits system, advice staff suggested that people were afraid to take up Tax Credits for fear of having to repay overpayments.

> 'People can be encouraged to make a transition to working formally by being given more information so that they know what help is available to them, particularly help with childcare, Tax Credits. People are unaware of what kind of support is on offer if they returned to work. The assumption is that if you find any work, you lose benefits full stop, which is misleading.' (Sue, 24, lone parent on New Deal)

Welfare to work

The current government has introduced a range of welfare-to-work programmes including the New Deal, which targets particular groups of people such as young people and lone parents. Over the past year (2005-06), Jobcentres have been replaced by new centres known as Jobcentre Plus. A raft of schemes has been tested to encourage people from benefits to work. One such scheme is the 'Back to Work Bonus'. People returning to work from benefits may receive up to £1,000 in place of benefits lost. Also available are job grants for claimants entering full-time work, who receive £100.

Another scheme is Work Trials, in which people over the age of 25 who are unemployed for over six months can take a job for up to 15 days and stay on benefits. Also, 'Twin Track', a pilot, is currently being run to allow people in Wales and North West England to earn while claiming benefits (CESI and Boundaries Unlimited, 2006). This scheme is currently undergoing evaluation. Extended payment of Housing Benefit and Council Tax Benefit, for four weeks after signing off Jobseeker's Allowance or Income Support has been made automatic. Although this may be effective in helping people to move into work, and overcoming a benefits trap in the short run, people will have to resume paying housing costs after this money runs out. Prospects of a sustained increase in wages or job progression are needed to make work pay.

In addition, schemes have been introduced to try to allay people's fears about returning to unstable jobs. One such scheme is Employment on Trial, where people can return to previous levels of Jobseeker's Allowance if they leave a job more than four weeks after starting. Provided this is correctly administered, this type of scheme may help to avert people from working and claiming without declaring income; and encourage people on benefits to take up formal opportunities.

The findings in the Newham study mirror those of a much larger qualitative survey of the Department for Work and Pensions' (DWP) 'Back to Work' programmes evaluated by the National Centre for Social Research (2001-2003), which looked at key elements of the back-to-work package examining the transitional period that occurs when people move into employment from benefits. The DWP identifies a range of barriers that persist towards the take-up of formal paid work, such as unfavourable views of the jobs available, a misunderstanding of the tax and benefits system, a distrust of official agencies, a fear of risks, short-term perspectives and narrow travel horizons and low aspirations (SEU, 2004). These all encourage people to work informally.

Benefits

The Welfare Reform Green Paper (DWP, 2006) could go further to improve the benefits system in relation to informal paid work. Current Earnings Disregard levels are set at very low levels, so that single people on benefits must declare earnings of over £5 per week.

At the same time, benefits levels are not set in line with income needed for acceptable living standards. This research suggests that policy from the Home Office that affects informal paid work should look at the setting of levels of NASS (National Asylum Support Service) support, the waiting times for the processing of asylum claims and the policy preventing people seeking asylum from taking-up paid work (see Chapter 9).

Support for small businesses

The Small Business Council, an advisory body to the Small Business Service of the Department of Trade and Industry, has published *Small business in the informal economy: Making the transition to the formal economy* (2005), a report examining the nature and impact of the informal economy on small businesses. A literature review detailing the evidence base was also undertaken. The government subsequently produced a formal response which affirmed the initial report and spoke of the need to 'Distinguish between the entrepreneurial and criminal elements of the informal economy and research, plan and act accordingly' (DTI, 2005, p 15). The report states that the 'Government seeks to strike the right balance between persuasion and deterrence, targeting particularly those operating wilfully in the informal economy' (p 15).

Regeneration initiatives promote micro-business but do not necessarily acknowledge that these industries may rely on informal paid work. These initiatives do not recognise making the transition from informal to formal paid work as a target (Smith, 2005). Some local interest is emerging in measuring the size and understanding the composition of the informal economy, including informal paid work. Several pilot projects are in progress to help people to legitimise their activity. These run on a regional level, with the support of national departments. Further details of projects such as the Her Majesty's Revenue and Customs North East Informal Economy Pilot and Bizfiz can be found in the CESI and Boundaries Unlimited (2006) report into informal activity in Merseyside. This activity is welcomed. However, much of it deals with the needs of small businesses and the self-employed rather than employees in informal paid work.

Deterrence

The Grabiner (2000) report is the most current comprehensive report on the informal economy. It stresses the importance of deterrence, and leads to a range of measures to combat benefit and tax fraud. It also acknowledges that there are people who work within the informal economy who would like to be legitimate, and includes recommendations such as setting up a confidential helpline; increased publicity; improved back-to-work programmes and amnesties. The report further suggests changing public attitudes to try to make informal work less socially acceptable. The recommendations set out in Chapter 9 put forward different approaches and ideas that may be more appropriate and effective in assisting people who undertake low-paid informal work to stay out of poverty.

Broadly speaking, current policy assumes that informal paid work is motivated by monetary gain, that is, out of greed, but not out of a genuine need for extra income. As a result, public policy responses attempt to deter this type of work by ensuring that the cost of punishment is greater than the benefit of participating (Williams et al, 2004b). However, for those who took part in this research, the rational decision to engage in informal paid work was made at the margin, where people have so little income to live on that the threat of being caught paled into insignificance compared to the threat of destitution, or debt and debt collectors.

9

Policy recommendations

Overview

The research findings in this study about the informal economy indicate that a fundamental change of approach is needed across the spectrum of welfare policy. The following recommendations call for a range of practical actions that could promote this change. They are drawn from a number of sources, including people engaged in low-paid informal work, related research studies, academics, think tanks, government officials, business people, and voluntary and community practitioners throughout the UK.

When the existence of the informal economy is acknowledged, it can introduce a new dimension to policy issues. For example, understanding the incentive structure for people on benefits looks very different when the option of informal work is added to the model. Therefore some recommendations suggest changes at the level of framing the problems and the solutions. Other changes involve setting new targets and integrating them into local and national policy aims.

In the shorter term, adjustments and additions to existing services could improve the system so that it works better for people who work within low-paid informal work. On their own, suggestions in this regard may be seen as 'tinkering at the edges'. Such small changes may be crucial for current service users but it is important that these are accompanied by more fundamental, longer-term changes to the benefits and tax system.

Changing attitudes and approaches

Need not greed

Policy and practice that deal with people who work informally should acknowledge the idea that everyone has a right to survive. If there are no accessible alternatives, then people may reasonably be expected to support themselves and their families through informal paid work. The tax and benefits systems should provide a smoother path to support people to make the transition from informal paid work to formal work.

Carrots not sticks

Measures should aim to help people who work informally to survive, to offer 'carrots', real routes out of poverty through formal working, while addressing some of the other issues affecting their lives, including housing, debt, skills, training and childcare. Where people take on informal paid work out of need, the decision about whether to risk being caught is different to that of someone who is avoiding taxes out of greed. For people in poverty the threat of the debt collector may be more pressing than that of being caught by the taxman. These people will not respond to threats, or 'sticks', because the alternative is a more immediate or severe threat.

Harnessing potential

The informal economy will continue to exist. Civil servants and politicians need to see the potential that it has to contribute more fully to our society. Rather than punish people for working informally and driving them further underground, alternatives should be developed that encourage and enable people to make the transition from informal to formal paid work. These may be people who have never had formal work and who live in communities where informal working is the norm; women without access to childcare; those who lack confidence and skills; and those arriving from overseas. Policymakers need to understand the stepping stones that people currently take from informal into formal work.

Delivering the goods

Policy may be most effectively delivered by forging deeper relationships with the voluntary and community sector, particularly in relation to harnessing the informal economy. Voluntary and community organisations are often working directly with people at a grass-roots level. Some are experienced and understand the problems that people face as well as already providing services to support them. They are well placed to develop policies and deliver work programmes to address the needs of local people and they are trusted more than government agencies.

Changing attitudes

In order for policy change to be successfully embedded, public and institutional attitudes must support this change. Rather than making informal paid work less socially acceptable, as suggested in the Grabiner (2000) report, the emphasis may be on promoting an understanding of the reasons why people undertake low-paid informal work.

Affordable living

Increase the national minimum wage

This study highlights the need to consider the decision that people make with respect to informal employment in the debate around minimum wage setting. It suggests that increasing, indexing and enforcing the minimum wage to ensure that those who work can afford the basic costs for survival may divert people from low-paid informal work. An estimated 1.1 million received an increase in wages in 2004 because they were working at the minimum wage (Low Wage Commission, 2004). There is evidence to suggest that many employers bypass the minimum wage legislation. The Living Wage Unit, based in the Greater London Assembly, recommends £6.70 per hour as a living wage for London.

Raise benefits levels

Benefits should be raised to allow people to cover basic living costs: Current levels of income, such as £55 a week for a single person on Jobseeker's Allowance, do not cover basic living costs such as healthy food, household products and the costs of looking for work such as travel and bills (Kempson, 1996).

Provide adequate childcare provision

Lack of childcare is a major barrier to formal employment. Informal flexible working is the only option for some. The solution is seen partly to lie in the generic provision of childcare and partly with employers having family-friendly policies. Models of universal provision, such as in Dundee where the local authority employs childcare workers, should be considered.

'There should be more incentives for people on benefits to get off them and find work. Family-friendly work environments, workplace crèches, are some of the issues that affect mothers when deciding to go back into work.' (Irene, 32, attended focus group with her baby)

Increase formal work opportunities

Better formal paid work options must be made available for people in deprived areas to win people over from the informal sector. Formal paid work may offer no more security of tenure than informal paid work; or may not offer pensions or wage progression. 'Making work pay' is not just about the wage rate, and in-work benefits, it is also about offering security of tenure, job progression and good, supportive working environments.

Changing rules and systems

Specific improvements could be made to the benefits and tax system and the asylum process to address the issue of low-paid informal work.

Changing the tax system

The tax system should not force people to choose between survival and informality. Either very low incomes should not be taxed, anything below £15-20,000, or the first band of one's personal tax allowance should rise to £12,000 per annum, for example. This could take millions out of the tax system and save a significant amount of money in terms of administrative costs.

One think-tank has suggested that under the present system, the government collects between £30 billion and £40 billion in Income Tax and National Insurance contributions from around 17 million households with incomes below £20,000 a year. Yet the government also distributes £30 billion to £40 billion in benefits to the same people. Cancellation of this overlap could be a step to take and so reduce the tax burden from 37% to 33% of national income (Warburton and Saatchi, 1999).

The benefits and tax threshold should be coordinated more closely, to smooth the transition from receiving benefits to progressing through a 'no benefits, no tax' point to paying tax.

A supportive tax system

The system could recognise and support employers who enable people to step across from the informal to the formal economy. Some work, currently considered informal, could be brought into the formal sphere through tax breaks for organisations or individuals. In addition, voluntary sector organisations should be allowed to employ people who are in receipt of benefits, on a casual basis, in work that benefits the local community.

Reform the Tax Credits system

The Tax Credits system remains an area in need of reform and simplification (Parliamentary Ombudsman, 2005) in order to ensure that Tax Credits alleviate poverty in low-paid work. Tax rebates or exemption from PAYE for those on the minimum wage might be considered. Including more parents on the borderline by changing thresholds for Tax Credits would be another option. Another way to rationalise the system would be to exclude Tax Credits as income in the calculation for entitlement to Housing Benefit. The recent changes announced in the Pre-Budget Report (HM Treasury, 2005) with regard to Tax Credit reassessments only if income levels go above £25,000 annually are welcomed. This was previously one of the drivers to informal paid work for those who would rather take the risk of not reporting than go through the complicated reassessment process.

Reducing delays in the process of applying for Tax Credits and allocating National Insurance numbers, and speeding up emergency payments that are currently reported to be difficult to obtain, as well as acting to ensure that the issue of overpayments is resolved without distress to the claimants, are some of the recommended measures to be taken (Newham Welfare Rights Action Group, 2005).

Simplify the benefits system

A careful and systematic reassessment of the benefits system is needed: The government acknowledges that 'The present benefits system for people of working age is too complex.... We need a simpler benefits system' (DWP, 2006, p 92). The current government pledges to rationalise the system: 'Benefits often overlap and have complex interactions with each other and Tax Credits. The next step is to review the range of benefits to identify the challenges to creating a single system with fair and effective solutions' (DWP, 2006, p 92). The National Audit Office also published a report in 2005 dealing with the complexity of the benefits system (NAO, 2005).

Raise basic benefits levels

Consideration should be given to setting basic benefits at a level that allows people to cover their basic cost of living. In addition, benefits should be index-linked either to earnings or inflation.

Extend the Housing Benefit run-on

Housing costs and Housing Benefit emerged as a crucial contributory issue to informal working and unemployment. Reform in this area is vital: 'Housing Benefit is often seen to undermine rather than underpin the wider goals of welfare reform.... Housing Benefit plays an essential role in underpinning the Government's wider goals of tackling poverty, promoting work for those who can, and addressing social exclusion' (DWP, 2006, p 82). Participants and advice staff recommended that the government significantly extend Housing Benefit run-on, and taper this to allow a smooth transition from unemployment to work.

> 'Government should allow claimants to keep some of the key benefits such as Housing Benefit when people get into low-paid work, rather than severing them off straight away and throwing them in at the deep end. When people get a job, you would want them to keep it, but if they face extreme difficulties including homelessness because they can't afford to rent, they may not keep the job, and sooner than later they will be on welfare again.' (Advice worker)

Understanding of work

The structures that deal with work, such as the Revenue & Customs and the Department for Work and Pensions operate on the tacit assumption that people have a shared understanding of the ideas around the concept of 'work'.

Our research indicates that there is variation around the ideas about work. People newly arriving in the UK may have a different understanding of work. The differences may be sharper among those arriving from developing countries. The different understandings of work may make people unresponsive to institutions that try to encourage people to participate in UK society and especially into formal paid work. It may render back-to-work services inaccessible.

For example, in some countries there is very little direct taxation; most revenue is taken from VAT. Therefore, some people arriving from these countries cannot be expected to be aware of the taxation system that operates here, and may not make a distinction between formal and informal work. For some people, the norms of work may be different, for example someone with a degree would not work in an unskilled job in their country. In some countries, jobs have different names, or jobs with the same names have different roles. This may also have an impact on the type of work people expect they will be able to do, and the reality of finding work.

A system that is sensitive to people's needs should recognise different types of diversity. The rules, systems and norms from a particular country may be a point of diversity as much as culture, language or shared experiences. If services are to be sensitive to diversity, and to reach out to people whom they often find hard to reach, they need to be able to deal with the idea that people have different norms and understandings of very fundamental concepts. Can we assume that people know how to search for jobs, that they know what a job agency is? Is this a norm in their country of origin? Services such as Jobcentre Plus or back-to-work organisations need to be clear about the idea that people may have preconceptions that they bring with them from their country of origin about what work is and isn't acceptable for someone with their qualifications to do.

Uncouple benefits

Currently, on losing Income Support, all other passport-ed benefits such as Housing Benefit, Council Tax benefit, free prescriptions and free school meals, are lost. This acts as a disincentive to taking low-paid formal jobs.

'Benefits should not be linked. If you lose Income Support, you lose all other passport-ed benefits such as Housing Benefit, Council Tax, free prescriptions, free school meals. It's too much to take in for some of our clients considering returning to work. They feel they wouldn't cope. Why not say 'ok you will lose this, but keep this benefit for the time being.' (Advice worker)

Increase the Earnings Disregard

Levels of Earnings Disregard – the amount of money one can earn while in receipt of benefits – which have remained virtually unchanged since 1988, should be raised and index-linked, enabling people to take transitional part-time or sessional jobs. Specific proposals on this include the following:

- Introduce an 'Earnings Credit' – the First Policy Action Team report (DfEE, 1999) recommended an Earnings Disregard reform using the Australian model of a £1,000 earnings credit pot.
- Establish a 'Community Allowance' scheme whereby local people on benefits are paid to provide key jobs to improve their community (Steele, 2006).
- The recent raising of Savings Disregard levels to £6,000 is welcomed (HM Treasury, 2005).

'The government says they encourage user involvement and participation, but rules are very restrictive on how to remunerate service users who are actually skilled and well versed with the kind of work we do. If we involve them more and pay them more than the expense limit, then we and the volunteers are obliged to declare. Service users do not want to declare bits of short work for fear of losing benefits. Even if we paid them a little more, they would still not be earning enough or getting the equivalent of their benefit level. We end up not being able to engage them constructively which would be beneficial to them, and to the organisation.' (Service user involvement officer)

Increase the efficiency of the benefits system

Inefficiencies in the benefits system can lead to delays, which lead to a build-up of debts. This has the knock-on effect of causing people to lose trust in the system. It is this lack of trust that benefits will be paid that can prevent people from taking the risk of going back to work.

The general issues around the poor administration and calculation of the 2003 Child Tax Credit and Working Tax Credit are widely documented. The Parliamentary Ombudsman's (2004) report noted 'technical problems which had led first to delays in payments, and then created other problems when the Revenue tried to remedy the situation by clawing back overpayments'. The report also noted that while for the majority of recipients the system appeared to be working, there was major concern for families on low incomes in particular in respect of the treatment and recovery of overpayment.

Link databases

Government agency database linkages should be made. The current separation between Revenue & Customs and the benefits agencies means that it is relatively easy for administrative error to occur in the payment of state benefits and the overpayment of Tax Credits or Housing Benefit run-on. Linkages may include, for example, showing a person's situation and therefore eligibility for Housing Benefit, Child Benefit, Working Tax

Credit and taxable income and/or taxes paid. This would also help reduce fraudulent claims.

Greater database unification would also facilitate a smooth transition from benefits to work. A system that can monitor and track the transition people make from benefits into work could respond immediately to changes and keep the right balance between benefits and tax, guaranteeing a basic income.

Staff training

Staff training in reforms to the benefits system is a key issue. Computer systems should make reforms such as Housing Benefit run-on, and automatic reclaim of benefits for people in temporary work, smooth. However, a clear understanding of policy by frontline delivery staff, to inform people of their entitlement and to reduce error, is needed to underpin this.

Changes to the tax and benefit system to encourage people back to work must be accompanied by efficient systems, staff training and regular information sharing. For example, while the current system allows one month of Housing Benefit run-on in order to encourage people back to work, in practice confusion between staff in the benefits agency and the Housing Benefit department means that run-on is not always allocated.

Alleviate debt

Measures relating to financial inclusion and education could be implemented to avert people from working informally when they face times of financial crisis. Tightening of the consumer credit regulations and support for people to build their savings and assets are needed. Staggered and deferred debt repayment for people leaving benefits would also be beneficial.

Improve systems for recently arrived workers

People seeking asylum should have the right to work. The asylum process is another example where introducing the informal economy into the picture strengthens call for reform. Genuine refugees wait for years before they are allowed to work due to delays in reaching decisions on the merits of asylum claims. During this time, these people may turn to informal paid work to survive.

The asylum process should be faster in its decision making: the time from application to determination of an asylum case can range from one to four years. During this time, people seeking asylum are expected to live solely on NASS (National Asylum Support Service) support, which is below the level of normal benefits, 70% of adult Income Support.

National Insurance number (NINo) rules should be clarified and more widely publicised: Changes in the NINo system are underway. However, there is a need to inform and educate employers and employees about the legal situation regarding the NINo. The general perception is that a person needs a NINo to begin work, and that the employer has to see a NINo card before they employ them. In fact some people are permitted to work while they await their NINo.

Harnessing hidden potential

There are those in low-paid informal work as well as the self-employed who have the skills and potential to make the transition, including launching their own businesses if there were a facilitating approach at both the national and local level to enable the legitimisation of such work.

Support teams for people in low-paid informal work

Specialised 'informal economy' transition and support teams should be set up by Revenue & Customs and the Department for Work and Pensions, throughout the regions, to advise and support individuals who are in low-paid informal work, to protect their rights and enable voluntary transition to formal work without fear of judgement or punishment.

These teams should also offer support to those who wish to remain in informal paid work until they are ready, as well as to those who wish to move into formal work. Such teams should be contracted-out to be run by voluntary and community sector organisations and/or enterprise agencies on behalf of Revenue & Customs and the Department for Work and Pensions. Many such organisations are already working with people who are working informally, giving them advice and support.

Increase the availability of formal work

Policy should target employers and attempt to stimulate the labour markets available to people in deprived areas. There are certain key industries where low-paid informal work takes place such as construction, home maintenance and repairs (internal and external), and caring. One of the main features of these industries is that work is contracted and sub-contracted. Therefore, work for employers such as the council, large supermarkets or hospitals ends up being carried out informally. This may reduce the formal alternatives as tasks that were once performed by people in formal jobs are undertaken by people employed informally. In certain industries, employers use self-employment status to avoid paying taxes and drive down wages, rendering minimum wage policy ineffective. The connection between sub-contracting and informality should be explored so that appropriate policies can be developed. It is vital that part-time, flexi-time or sessional work that people can fit around their childcare responsibilities or health needs is made more widely available. In addition, in-work benefits such as good pension schemes, private health insurance and so on can encourage movement into formal employment.

Increase support with formal job search

People need support in looking for work, so that it is as easy to find formal job opportunities as it is to find informal ones. These include:

- Borough-wide diversity and equal opportunities teams could use outreach workers to gather and disseminate news about potential formal jobs into communities where there is known to be high levels of informal working, accessing local networks.
- An outreach worker could engage people working informally and offer them training or assistance around the application process.
- Those who have been in low-paid informal work for any length of time may have low confidence and lack self-esteem, as well as other needs, when applying for and starting formal paid work. There is scope for support and advice, possibly provided by

a mentor, to help people to overcome these issues and fears, alongside more practical support.

- Information about informal work is passed through language groups, cultural, ethnic and other community groups, as people offer each other support through these networks. These networks could be harnessed to spread information about formal work opportunities.

- Some innovative local-level initiatives do acknowledge that agencies which provide access to formal jobs do not reach all people within certain parts of local communities. In Newham, for example, housing officers have been employed to reach out to people who were not accessing formal jobs and provide them with information and support.

- Given the local and regional differences that are likely in the nature and composition of informal paid work, local-level solutions, or national solutions tailored to local need, may be the most effective approach to assisting people working within low-paid informal work.

- Another example is a one-stop-shop, which has been opened in Bradford enabling visitors to obtain information about council services, tax and benefits, and a range of other issues. It is run in partnership by Bradford Council, Revenue & Customs, Jobcentre Plus, the National Health Service, Citizens Advice Bureaux and the police.

Increase access to formal work

The initiative should be taken by employers, government agencies and the voluntary and community sector to:

- work with recruitment agencies on reaching out to those who are in low-paid informal work;
- encourage employers to provide work experience to people who do not have UK work experience;
- explore new types of volunteering opportunities and internships with the voluntary sector and with business that are flexible to the needs and timetables of individuals, and enable people to fit voluntary work experience around earning a living to support themselves;
- increase provision of English lessons for overseas doctors, lawyers and so on, so that they may have the best chance of accessing jobs within their profession and do not have to turn to informal work. (Such lessons are run by a number of organisations including the Refugee Council.) English classes could be organised around language groups, so that teachers with specific foreign language skills could be found. This could be within a working environment within their profession;
- register qualifications and skills from abroad and ensure that they are accredited. Again increased information about people's qualification and transferable skills should be spread to employers. It should be significantly cheaper to invest in converting a doctor's qualifications to meet UK standards than training someone without previous experience. The UK National Recognition Information Centre for the United Kingdom is the official information provider on the comparability of international qualifications from over 180 countries worldwide.

'Government should require recruitment agencies and all employers to preserve jobs that require less communication in English for non-English speakers ... they should seek out those who have a language barrier and offer support.' (Charlie, 41)

'English tuition should be available in all the areas, easy, approachable and free and they should be advertised in all the languages using mass media such as TV, radio, newspaper and leaflets, so that everyone is aware of it.' (Naila, 32)

Corporate social responsibility

The existing relationship between informal employers and employees could be used more effectively to access and support people:

- The Revenue & Customs local business development teams should be increased in number, capacity and resources, as there is a great deal of scope for large and small employers to assist employees into formal work.
- Smaller employers may need support to move employees into legitimacy (Copisarow and Barbour, 2004).
- Specific industries known to employ more people in low-paid informal work should be targeted, to support them to create more economically viable formal opportunities for both themselves as employer and the employees. Achieving this in the construction and domestic consumer services would deal with 85% of all informal work (SBC, 2004).
- CESI and Boundaries Unlimited (2006) point to Formalisation Voucher schemes in a number of European Community countries, which use a voucher system to encourage employers to use formal rather than informal labour, as models of good practice.
- An initiative should be established that is equivalent to 'Pathfinders to Work', designed to test ways in which people can be supported to make the transition from informal to formal paid work.
- Large industries which use subcontracting and notional self-employment to avoid minimum wage and rights responsibilities towards their employees should be more tightly controlled.
- Experience from other countries should be given consideration when developing informal economy support programmes in the UK. For example, in Belgium people in receipt of social benefit allowance are entitled to work for up to six months while retaining this allowance as a part of a scheme run in partnership with 600 registered businesses (CESI and Boundaries Unlimited, 2006).

Information and education

A national information campaign should be delivered to raise awareness of the advantages of formal work; the disadvantages of informal work; and the role of the tax and benefit systems.

National information campaign

A range of methods including non-traditional techniques should be used to reach those people who may be harder to access. These may include:

- spreading information locally about organisations who work with people who are working informally, through schools, doctors' surgeries, the voluntary and community sector, and public sector services, such as Jobcentre Plus;
- using nationwide networks of community groups to help disseminate information about benefits and signpost where support is available for making the transition into formal work;
- devising advertising campaigns delivered through the media, including the tabloid press, the internet, emails, that show the advantages of working formally;
- training new arrivals to the UK in their rights as workers might help to avoid exploitation due to a lack of awareness;
- raising awareness through community networks, through planned activities such as training or information events, or more ad-hoc methods such as 'word of mouth';

- publicising successful outcomes in the local media. This would help to change perceptions and build more positive attitudes;
- using a mix of outreach as well as leafleting campaigns. Community language radio and television stations could be used. Also using as many of the local languages as possible and working with the gatekeepers, those who hold positions of trust, within community groups, to devise and run the campaigns;
- running borough-wide targeted poster campaigns, featured on public transport and in the local press, setting out the benefits of working formally.

'The government should devise a way of reaching out to people in need and the hard to reach may not necessarily be expected to read newspapers or pay attention to TV promotional. There should be outreach programmes to find them wherever they may be.' (Focus group participant)

Introduce a National Schools Programme

A lot more could be done at earlier stages to influence the behaviour and attitudes of young people before they enter the world of work. The national curriculum (from year seven) needs to be developed to include 'the world of work' for the general education of all children in the UK.

A compulsory school curriculum module on the world of work including the benefits of formal working and the tax and benefit system should be developed that could be adapted to be locally relevant. It would be equally important to ensure that teachers know of the potential benefits of selecting this module within personal, health and social education lessons to begin with, but move towards making this a core subject.

Increased partnerships with local businesses, the public sector and schools to promote work experience opportunities would increase school children's understanding about the world of work.

'I think schools should have compulsory career-advising lessons, where students are taught how to correctly approach employers.' (Focus group participant)

'We need more organisations that help young people to find work. If these organisations are in place, they need more advertising, I am not aware of them.' (Focus group participant)

Further research

There is a recognised body of academic research that has been conducted into the UK's informal economy. Developing practical solutions that can be tested does not need to wait for all possible research on the informal economy to be completed. However, research would be valuable in the following areas as there is a huge potential for understanding more about the informal economy, and refining policy around the issue for social benefit.

- *Informal employers:* taking a closer look at the informal economy from the perspective of employers. A study to collect systematic evidence relating to the attitudes, perceptions and recruitment practices of employers, covering the labour and skill needs of different types of enterprises across a range of sectors.
- *Background, culture and informal employment:* looking at people's experience and understanding of work from a cross-cultural and cross-country perspective;

understanding how these perspectives may impact on attitude to formality and informality in work, and to the benefits system.

- *Routes out of the informal economy:* talking to people who have made the transition into the formal economy, for whom informal working is in the past. Looking at the routes out of informal working that have worked, and trying to understand how these may be replicated and which types of organisation should deliver them.

- *Informal money:* looking at how money earned informally is spent and the impact of the informally earned cash on the local area. Understanding spending patterns where money is earned informally and building a true picture of the economic impact of informal work on a local area.

- *Housing and informal working:* exploring connections between housing and informal paid work, and understanding informal work as a consequence of high housing costs; the interrelationship between housing and labour markets and the influence of the allocation processes within social housing.

- *Impact of privatisation and sub-contracting on the informal economy:* examining the effect that privatisation, particularly sub-contracting, has had on low-paid informal work, and the relationship and disconnection between employer and employees. Review Europe-wide schemes engaging employers in assisting people from informal to formal employment, and scope further UK pilots.

- *Survey attitudes of children and young people:* understanding the attitudes, motivations and circumstances of children and young people in relation to formal and informal paid work. This would explore learnt behaviour patterns of generational employment habits.

10

Conclusion

Bringing people into the formal sphere, either by redefining their work as formal or by allowing them to develop their strengths and access formal paid work, would have a range of positive effects. For example, in the long run, it would enable people to find routes out of poverty and therefore reduce dependency on benefits.

Specific policy on the informal economy needs to be developed. There is currently no overarching strategy that cuts across government departments to address the informal economy. Low-paid informal work continues to be viewed as benefit fraud and/or tax evasion without a good understanding of the reasons behind it. There is much to be gained from looking at where informal paid work helps people to resist poverty, and from helping people on low incomes to make the transition to formal paid work.

Current welfare policy often seems to assume that those living in poor communities experience a world of nine-to-five work, where those who are without formal work may live on benefits and engage in job search, and perhaps voluntary work, until they find formal work which will support them. In reality, it often does not seem possible to survive on benefits, for some it is extremely difficult to engage in job search, there are alternative ways to top-up income, and not everyone can find formal work which pays a living wage.

In some cases the system creates significant disincentives to enter formal paid work. While the theory suggests that returning to work can lead to a better life, in reality, returning to work for people in poverty can mean coping with huge debts and a much harder struggle to cover basic costs, leaving people both time-poor and money-poor; and reinforcing the 'benefits trap'.

There is need for action now if these issues are going to be tackled. Unless there is cohesion and coordinated action by government, the voluntary sector and other stakeholders, low-paid informal work will continue and those involved will remain poor and on the fringes of society.

Responsibility and good citizenship promoted by government derives from vibrant communities. If conditions of extreme deprivation including child poverty persist in deprived neighbourhoods, accompanied by a lack of legitimate opportunities to escape from them, low-paid informal work will persist as well.

References

ALG (Association of London Government) (2004) *ALG Homelessness Working Group: Temporary to permanent accommodation initiatives in London*: London: ALG.

BOND (British Overseas NGOs for Development) End Child Poverty Coalition, Oxfam and Trades Union Congress (TUC) (2005) *Making UK poverty history*, London: BOND/End Child Poverty Coalition/Oxfam/TUC.

Brewer, M., Goodman, A., Shaw, J. and Sibieta, L. (2006) *Poverty and inequality in Britain*, London: Institute for Fiscal Studies.

Burchardt, T. and Le Grand, J. (2002) *Constraint and opportunity: Identifying voluntary non-employment*, London: Centre for Analysis of Social Exclusion, London School of Economics and Political Science.

CAB (Citizen's Advice Bureau) (2003) *Serious benefits*, London: CAB.

CESI (Centre for Economic and Social Inclusion) and Boundaries Unlimited (2006) *The informal economy in Merseyside*, London: Merseyside Entrepreneurship Commission.

Copisarow, R. and Barbour, A. (2004) *Self-employed people in the informal economy: Cheats or contributors?*, London: Community Links.

CPAG (Child Poverty Action Group) (2005) *Shaping the Incapacity Benefit reforms Green Paper*, London: CPAG (www.cpag.org.uk).

CPAG (2005) *First steps to reform tax credits*, London: CPAG.

DfEE (Department for Education and Employment) (1999) *Jobs for all: Report of the Policy Action Team for Jobs – PAT 1*, London: Cabinet Office.

Dorsett, R., Finlayson, L., Ford, R., Marsh, A., White, M. and Zarb, G. (1998) *Leaving Incapacity Benefit*, DSS Report No 86, Leeds: Corporate Document Services.

DTI (Department of Trade and Industry) (2005) *Government response to the Small Business Council report on the informal economy*, London: The Stationery Office.

DTLR (Department for Transport, Local Government and the Regions) (2001) *Strong local leadership: Quality public services*, White Paper, London: The Stationery Office.

DWP (Department for Work and Pensions) (2006) *A new deal for welfare: Empowering people to work*, Welfare Reform Green Paper, London: DWP.

Engberson, G. (2001) *Controlling a new migration world*, London/New York, NY: Routledge.

Evans, Y., Herbert, J., Datta, K., May, J., McIlwaine, C. and Wills, J. (2005) *Making the city work: Low-paid employment in London*, London: Queen Mary, University of London.

FSA (Financial Services Authority) (2004) *Financial risk outlook 2004*, London: FSA (www.fsa.org.uk).

GLA (Greater London Authority) (2001) *Refugees and asylum seekers in London*, London: GLA.

GLA (2005) *A fairer London: The living wage in London*, London: GLA.

Grabiner, Lord (2000) *The informal economy: A report by Lord Grabiner QC*, London: The Stationery Office.

Gravonetter, M. (1983) *The strength of weak ties: A network theory revisited*, New York, NY: State University of New York, Stony Brook.

Griggs, J., McAllister, F. and Walker, R. (2005) *The new tax credits system: Knowledge and awareness among recipients*: One Parent Families/Roger Carlsson Foundation

Hannan, C. (1999) *Beyond networks: Social cohesion and unemployment exit rates*, ILR Working Paper 028, Colchester: University of Essex, Institute for Labour Research.

HM Treasury (2005) *Britain meeting the global challenge: Enterprise, fairness and responsibility. Pre-Budget report 2005*, London: The Stationery Office.

ILO (International Labour Organization) (2002) *Decent work and the informal economy, Report VI*, International Labour Conference, 90th Session, Geneva: ILO.

Jordan, B. and Duvell, F. (2002) *The dilemmas of transnational mobility*, Cheltenham: Edward Elgar.

Kempson, E. (1996) Life on a low income, York: Joseph Rowntree Foundation.

Labour Party (2005) *The Labour Party Manifesto 2005: Britain forward not back*, London: Labour Party.

LBN (London Borough of Newham) (2005) *Focus on Newham, local people and local conditions*, London: LBN.

Lister, R. (2005) *Poverty*, Cambridge: Polity Press.

Living Wage Unit (2005) *Poverty pay hits one in seven Londoners*, London: London Citizens.

Low Wage Commission (2004) *Protecting young workers: The National Minimum Wage*, London: The Stationery Office.

NAO (National Audit Office) (2005) *Department for Work and Pensions: Dealing with the complexity of the benefits system*, London: The Stationery Office (www.nao.org.uk/ publications/nao_reports/05-06/0506592.pdf).

Newham Welfare Rights Action Group (2005) 'Tax credits: experiences of Newham claimants', London: unpublished.

North, D., Ramsden, M., Birch, J. and Sanderson, I. (2004) *Rethink: Barriers to employment in Newham*, London: LBN.

ONS (Office for National Statistics) (2001) *Census 2001* (www.statistics.gov.uk/census2001/ census2001.asp).

Ormerod, P. and Smith, L. (1999) *Job search, unemployment and the topology of social networks*, London: Voltera.

Palmer, G., Carr., J. and Kenway, P. (2005) *Monitoring poverty and social exclusion*, York: Joseph Rowntree Foundation.

Parliamentary Ombudsman (2005) *Tax credits: Putting things right*, London: The Stationery Office.

Penrose, J. (2002) *Poverty and asylum in the UK*, London: Oxfam/Refugee Council.

Pfau-Effinger, B. (2003) 'Development of informal work in Europe: causal factors, problems, approaches to solutions', Paper presented at EU Workshop 'Informal/ undeclared work: research on its changing nature and policy strategies in an enlarged Europe', Brussels, 21 May (ftp.//cordis.lu/pub/improving/does_conf/work_pfau-effinger.pdf).

Refugee Council (2004) *Information service: The information survival kit for anyone working with asylum seekers and refugees*, London: Refugee Council Information Services.

Renooy, P.H. and Mateman, S. (2001) *Undeclared labour in Europe: Towards an integrated approach of combating undeclared labour: Final report*, Amsterdam: Regioplan.

Renooy, P., Ivarsson, S., van der Wusten-Gristoi, O. and Meijer, E. (2004) *Undeclared work in an enlarged Union*, Brussels: European Commission.

Ridge, T. (2000) *Childhood poverty and social exclusion: From a child's perspective*, Bristol: The Policy Press.

Robinson, D., Dunn, K. and Ballintyne, S. (1998) *Social Enterprise Zones: Building innovation into regeneration*, York: Joseph Rowntree Foundation.

SBC (Small Business Council) (2004) *Small businesses in the informal economy: Making the transition to the formal economy*, London: The Stationery Office.

SEU (Social Exclusion Unit) (1998) *Bringing Britain together: A national strategy for neighbourhood renewal*, London: SEU.

SEU (2004) *Stimulating jobs and enterprise in deprived communities*, London: The Stationery Office.

Smerdon, M. and Robinson, D. (2004) *Enduring change: The experience of the Community Links Social Enterprise Zone: Lessons learnt and next steps*, Bristol/York: The Policy Press/ Joseph Rowntree Foundation.

Smith, D. (2000) 'Dealed out? Welfare to work and social exclusion', *Local Economy*, vol 15, no 4, pp 312-24.

Smith, D. (2005) *On the margins of inclusion: Changing labour markets and social exclusion in London*, Bristol: The Policy Press.

Steele, J. (2006) *The CREATE proposal*, London: British Urban Regeneration Association.

Tilly, C. (1990) 'Transplanted networks', in V. Yans-McLaughlin (ed) *Immigration reconsidered: History, sociology and politics*, Oxford University Press, pp 70-95.

Travers, A. (2001) *Prospects for enterprise: An investigation into the motives of workers in the informal economy*, London: Community Links.

Travers, J. and Jordan, B. (2000) 'The motivations of informal economic workers', Research brief, Unpublished.

Vasta, E. (2004) *Informal employment and immigrant networks: A review paper*, Centre on Migration, Policy and Society Working Paper No. 2, Oxford: University of Oxford.

Warburton, P. and Saatchi, M. (1999) *The war of independence*, London: Centre for Policy Studies.

Williams, C. and Windebank, J. (1998) *Informal employment in the advanced economies: Implications for work and welfare*, London: Routledge.

Williams, C. and Windebank, J. (2002) 'The uneven geographies of informal economic activities: A case study of two British cities', *Work, Employment and Society*, vol 16, pp 231-50.

Williams, C. and Windebank, J. (2004a) 'The heterogeneity of the underground economy', *International Journal of Economic Development*, vol 6, no 2.

Williams, C. and Windebank, J. (2004b) 'Beyond deterrence: rethinking the UK public policy approach towards undeclared work', *Public Policy and Administration*, vol 19, no 1, Spring.

Wolk, S. and Foster, T. (2003) 'Rocketing in a hard place', *London Housing*, October.

Further references

A full bibliography of texts relating to all aspects of the informal economy can be found on the Community Links website (www.community-links.org.uk).

Appendix A
Research methodology

Literature search

A search of literature was undertaken to identify relevant material in the UK and internationally. Sources searched included electronic databases, existing reviews and bibliographies as well as direct contact with experts in the field. On the international perspective, the European Union, the Organisation for Economic Co-operation and Development and International Labour Organisation were the key sources used.

Literature review

Key documents from the literature search were selected and appraised. A draft review paper was produced relating literature to research questions and identifying key issues, knowledge gaps and potential case studies. One of the authors presented interim findings for discussion at an international conference organised by the European Microfinance Network in Barcelona.

Approach

The 'What if...?' approach holds the experiences and views expressed by individuals to be central in debate about service delivery. Therefore a phenomenological approach to the research was considered appropriate. It was decided to undertake one-to-one interviews with people engaged in informal paid work and on low incomes, to capture the voices of those individuals.

Sample size

The initial sample size was 50 individuals. As there is little existing research exploring perspectives of low-paid informal work in the UK, it was felt that the interviewing had not reached saturation at this sample size. Therefore it was decided to undertake a further 50 interviews. Another reason for using a larger sample size was to ensure variation within the sample. A total of 100 interviews were conducted before it was felt that most of the issues had been uncovered.

Sample

The aim of the research project was to collect the perspectives of employees on low incomes in the informal economy. A snowball sampling technique was used, where each participant was asked to suggest the next participant from among people they knew. The intention was to include in the sample a wide range of people in low-paid informal work and on low incomes (the minimum wage and below) according to gender, ethnicity, age and employment. In this way, the widest possible range of issues and attitudes could be described and analysed. Interviews were periodically reviewed to ensure that the sample reflected a wide variation across the demographic profile of Newham.

Recruitment

The snowball sampling technique made use of a range of starting points. In this way, it was hoped to capture a wide range of views, and to avoid a bias that may be created by starting the snowball from only one point. The starting points included:

- local residents already in contact with the Community Links 'What if...?' Team, with Community Links advice workers and outreach workers;
- local residents in contact with other organisations working within the community, including employment support agencies, local voluntary and community organisations and faith groups;
- leaflets and posters in advice centres, doctors' surgeries, post offices, libraries and leisure centres;
- advertisements for research participants placed in the local newspaper *The Newham Recorder*.

Confidentiality

Confidentiality was guaranteed by asking respondents to suggest names by which they wanted to be known in this research. Interviews were not tape recorded due to the nature of the subject matter but detailed notes were taken. It was felt that potential respondents would be put off from participating in the research if evidence of their illegal activity was stored on tape.

Local researchers

The ethnic diversity of Newham was a key characteristic considered in the recruitment of interviewers. Applicants had to be from the local community and able to speak another language as well as English.

The project was led by an experienced researcher and interviewer within the 'What if...?' Team. Local researchers went through a normal recruitment process, responding to advertisements placed locally and were selected on the basis of their experience, interpersonal skills and the second languages spoken. Drawn from the local community they were fairly well versed with local issues including the benefits system and aspects of the informal economy in general. Some of them had personal experiences of low-paid informal work.

The team drew on Community Links' networks to recruit from under-represented communities. No Bangladeshi interviewers responded to our advertisements. Volunteers from other Asian communities conducted the interviews within the Bangladeshi community.

Volunteers received in-house training at Community Links, which covered health and safety issues, the definition of the informal economy, understanding the benefits system, interviewing and information-recording skills, ethical issues including 'informed consent', confidentiality as well as cultural sensitivities in the local community. Additionally, interviewers received one-and-a-half days training from the British Market Research Bureau (BMRB) on principles of qualitative research and interviewing techniques. The researchers received £50 per interview conducted.

Discussion of recruitment

Researchers observed that the most effective starting point was community organisations; the leaflets were the least effective starting point. Each person interviewed was asked to pass on cards with interviewers' contact details to others engaged in low-paid informal work.

It is likely that Community Links' reputation, with a one in three brand recognition in Newham engendered trust and made it easier for the team of volunteers to be identified as 'working for a local charity'. It is probable that interviewees would not have spoken so candidly about their informal paid work to officials from local or central government agencies.

After the collection of the initial 50 interviews, an incentive of £30 was introduced to speed up the recruitment process. This proved effective and the following interviews were conducted within one month.

Interviews

Overall, 100 interviews were conducted in one-to-one sessions lasting 45 minutes to one hour. Profiling data was captured on age, gender, ethnicity, and location of interview. Based on the 'What if...?' research approach and utilising our previous research experience on this issue, investigative tools including a topic guide for semi-structured interviews and a discussion guide for focus groups were designed.

Each interview was conducted one-to-one in a space that the interviewee chose and felt comfortable in. Interviews were conducted only with those who answered affirmatively to the first question 'have you at any time worked off the books, cash-in-hand or accepted money for work while receiving benefits?' Other questions explored issues such as:

- their personal circumstances;
- how participants defined informal paid work;
- how they thought their informal paid work impacted on themselves, their families and their communities;
- their motivation/reasons for working in this way;
- their aspirations for the future;
- their knowledge of other options available to them, or how they would go about finding out about options;
- the barriers and challenges they identified in making the transition into formal employment;
- practical ideas for supporting their transition to formal employment.

Interviewees came across as being honest about what they reported, and the fact that they came forward voluntarily well aware of the nature of the research mainly through the snowball introductions adds to the veracity of their stories. But the main issue interviewers had to contend with was the raised expectation of respondents on what the research would contribute towards change of their circumstances. Questions like, what's in this for me? Will this research make any impact on my personal circumstances? What's the difference between this and many other surveys carried out in the borough with no improvement to services? Will this research help me get out of temporary housing, get a better job, sort out my childcare issues or immigration status? These were all raised during the course of the research.

The researchers, however, were under clear instructions not to promise anything apart from the fact that the research would bring all the issues raised to the fore, and inform policymakers both at a local and national level in a report. Interviewees keen on reading the report when it was published, left their emails or telephone contacts with the researchers. They were also invited to focus groups.

Focus groups

Four focus groups were held to discuss and develop the ideas recommended by research participants who had taken part in the interviews. Two of these were with the research participants themselves, and a further two were with practitioners and policymakers. Issues in recruiting people to the focus groups were mainly in finding an appropriate time that suited everyone involved for these to go ahead, so that people could fit them in around childcare and work needs. At one of the focus groups a child was admitted to enable the parent to attend. The focus groups each consisted of between six and 12 people.

All the issues arising from the research were laid out on flip charts and participants were invited to suggest solutions. These were also noted and later discussed with practitioners and policymakers who were also invited to suggest solutions and innovative ways of overcoming some of the identified issues. They form part of the policy recommendations in this report.

Project Advisory Group (PAG)

The project had an advisory group of 10 members. Participation was voluntary and membership was drawn from varied backgrounds in the voluntary and community sector, business and academia. The group was chaired by a senior research manager from the Joseph Rowntree Foundation.

The role of the PAG was to advise, support and help with specific aspects of the project, for example by providing information and contacts or informing on policy and practice as well as reviewing the progress of the project. The meetings also provided an opportunity to focus on planning for the outputs and dissemination of findings. The group met twice and at the last meeting agreed to carry on in this advisory role beyond the span of the project in order to help build a UK-wide informal economy campaign network and to formulate a dissemination strategy.

Data analysis

Data was coded. Data codes were cross-referenced by two researchers. Descriptive and axial coding was undertaken to build theories of behaviour within the given context according to the descriptions and narratives offered in the text. Using a grounded theory approach, these theories, internal to the text, were developed and cross-checked by further reading of the text and discussion. Where possible, the theory was cross-checked with existing data sources and theories to triangulate the hypotheses in order to build towards the detailed recommendations presented.

Appendix B
Overview of core research area: London Borough of Newham

Population

The London Borough of Newham has a population of 244,291 (ONS, 2001). This is the 11th largest compared with all other London boroughs. Half the residents are under 30 years of age. The borough is one of the most ethnically diverse in the UK: 65.2% black and minority ethnic communities to 34.8% white British. There are over 100 different languages spoken in the borough.

Deprivation

Newham was ranked 11 out of 324 most deprived boroughs in England and Wales, and the third most deprived borough in London after Tower Hamlets and Hackney (Index of Multiple Deprivation, 2004).[3] Half of the adult population and two thirds of the children living in Newham are regarded as living in poverty based on Newham Household Panel Surveys (2004-05).[4]

Economic activity

The proportion of economically active population in Newham is lower (61%) than both the London region (74%) and Britain (78%). The level of unemployment (9.5%) is twice as high as Britain's overall level. 11.4% of Newham residents say they have never worked compared with 4.7% of London residents.

Housing

Newham is densely populated: the average number of people per square kilometre is 7,013 while in the London region the figure is 4,647 and in England it is 380. 40.2% of Newham residents are in receipt of Housing Benefit (LBN, 2005, p 58), which is twice the proportion of England and Wales.

---

3 www.odpm.gov.uk/pub/446/Indicesofdeprivation2004revisedPDF2198Kb_id1128446.pdf

4 www.newham.info/research/NHPS.htm

Health

According to the 2001 Census, 16% of residents of working age in Newham reported having a limiting long-term illness. This proportion is higher than in the London region and England and Wales, 12% and 13.5% respectively.

Asylum seekers

Newham has the second highest number of asylum seekers (3,207) in London, after Haringey; and they represent 1.3% of the total population of Newham. The number of refugees and asylum seekers in London at the end of 2000 was estimated at between 352,000 and 422,000. Of these, 80% live on NASS (National Asylum Support Services) payments (GLA, 2001).

The future for Newham and East London

There are a plethora of proposed major developments for East London including Stratford City, the Olympics sites, and the regeneration of the Thames Gateway area. New infrastructure, new businesses and thousands of new homes have begun to transform the landscape. It is important to note, however, that this regeneration activity may not necessarily change the circumstances of local residents engaged in low-paid informal work although it may generate more informal work.

Informal paid work in Newham

There is no data with which to estimate the number of Newham residents in low-paid informal work. Anecdotal evidence suggests high levels of informal economic activity within the borough. The London Boroughs of Newham and Haringey have recently commissioned the Community Links 'What if...?' Team to quantify the size of the informal economy in these respective boroughs. Similar exercises at ward level have been carried out by Professor Colin Williams in Nottinghamshire, Sheffield and Southampton (Williams and Windebank, 2004a). These are the only instances on record for attempting to quantify the size of the informal economy in specific localities in the UK.

Appendix C
Community Links and the Community Links 'What if...?' Team

Community Links

Community Links is an innovative charity running community-based projects in East London. Founded in 1977, we now help over 53,000 vulnerable children, young people and adults every year, with most of our work delivered in Newham, one of the poorest boroughs in Europe. Our successes influence both community-based organisations nationwide and government policy. See www.community-links.org or email uk@community-links.org for more information.

Community Links 'What if...?' Team

> Unless and until we can find new ways of using mainstream budgets to tackle multiple deprivation, we will always be tinkering at the edges. (Robinson et al, 1998, p 2)

The Community Links 'What if...?' Team (formerly the Social Enterprise Zone [SEZ]) has succeeded in securing 12 national policy changes and has successfully tested 11 ideas for improving delivery of local services since 1999. The idea for a SEZ was developed in 1996 as a proposal to tackle generations of poverty and disadvantage. Its name reflected the principles behind a 'Business Enterprise Zone' model, which was fashionable in the 1980s, for example Canary Wharf, where 'statutory regulations had been relaxed to make (an) area more attractive to business. The SEZ would be an area freed from a range of statutory regulations and controls ... in which local agencies would be given the powers to bend the rules blocking regeneration.... No rule should be inviolable if a genuine case could be made for changing it' (Smerdon and Robinson, 2004, p 3).

Today the 'What if...?' Team continues to realise the original objectives of ensuring that the needs of people in Newham are met through efficient and effective use of public resources and services; and to make the case for national policy changes, which arise from this practical experience. The 'What if...?' Team's innovative, non-political approach has proved to be very effective in working with local public sector services, like local Jobcentres and schools, to help them identify problems and barriers blocking performance and efficiency; to gather ideas and solutions from users and staff; and then develop and run practical projects to test these ideas.

Some ideas are simple and practical and can be implemented locally, for example, setting up an independent disability benefits helpline or a form filling and interpreting service in local Jobcentres and Social Security offices. Others require central government support and changes to rules – these form the basis of our contributions to policy development, for example, developing new solutions to existing government programmes that support the unemployed into self-employment.

For in-depth information about the Community Links 'What if...?' Team please refer to:

- Smerdon, M. and Robinson, D. (2004) *Enduring change: The experience of the Community Links Social Enterprise Zone: Lessons learnt and next steps*, Bristol/York: The Policy Press/Joseph Rowntree Foundation.
- Robinson, D., Dunn, K. and Ballintyne, S. (1998) *Social Enterprise Zones: Building innovation into regeneration*, York: Joseph Rowntree Foundation.

The Community Links 'What if...?' Team's previous work on the informal economy

- **2000**: Community Links' SEZ (now known as Community Links 'What if...?' Team) worked in East London with Dr Andrew Travers, Exeter University, to understand local people's motivations and circumstances for working informally (Travers, 2001) This highlighted the positive aspects of informality such as working for a living; the pride, self-esteem and self-worth that is derived from providing for one's family; and an understanding about certain barriers, such as the benefits/poverty trap, which pushes people into low-paid informal work.
- **2000/01**: Two Public Attitude Surveys were conducted in Stratford, Newham and Oxford Street, Central London. Responses showed that the public are surprisingly tolerant of people who work informally, in contrast with the dominant government view that these people are criminals.
- **2002/03**: Work in partnership with the Inland Revenue on a 'Tax Credit take-up' project with 'hard-to-reach' groups confirmed SEZ's earlier findings in practice – namely that people working informally cannot benefit from or access government initiatives such as Tax Credits and the national minimum wage.
- **2003/04**: Discussions with the Inland Revenue about these findings prompted SEZ to join forces with Street (UK), a micro finance charity, to host an Inland Revenue Senior Inspector from the Cross-Cutting Policy Team for six months on secondment. Her task was to understand people's motivations, perceptions, attitudes and circumstances for working informally by interviewing Community Links' and Street (UK)'s clients.
- **2003/04**: HMRC created a new central compliance team including a unit focusing specifically on the informal economy. As a result, pilots were set up in the regions to aid the transition of small businesses to formal trading.
- **2003/04**: Community Links was invited to contribute to the Social Exclusion Unit's research into stimulating jobs and enterprise in deprived neighbourhoods (SEU, 2004); and to the Small Business Council's review of the informal economy (SBC, 2004). Many of our recommendations were incorporated.
- **2004 (September)**: SEZ co-authored with Street (UK) a report (Copisarow and Barbour, 2004) that examined the evidence, implications and policy recommendations for small businesses trading informally. It was widely distributed, received extensive press coverage and has helped to influence government policy development.

continued.../

- **2004 (November)**: The 'What if...?' Team launched a three-year campaign to bring about change for those employed informally but who want to make the transition to the formal economy. It was apparent that in order to embark on this task we needed to carry out on the ground research, focusing on those employed informally, and investigating people's aspirations and barriers and to explore what those involved proposed as *practical solutions* to make the transition.

Also available from The Policy Press
Published in association with the Joseph Rowntree Foundation

Child poverty in large families
*Jonathan Bradshaw, Naomi Finch, Emese Mayhew,
Veli-Matti Ritakallio and Christine Skinner*

The UK child poverty rate for large families is among the highest in the OECD. This study investigates the prevalence and characteristics of poor children in large families in the UK and how we compare with other countries. It also explores how the tax and benefit system has varied by family size over recent years and how this in turn compares with other countries. Given the UK government's commitment to the abolition of child poverty by 2020, the report discusses how the tax and benefit system might be adapted in favour of large families so that this target might be achieved.

The work is based on the secondary analysis of national and international data. The national data sets included the Family Resources Survey, The Millennium Cohort Study and the Family and Child Survey. The international data was drawn from the European Community Household Panel and the Luxembourg Income Study. The study also drew on national and international data on how the tax benefit system impacts on model families.

Paperback £12.95 US$25.95

ISBN-10 1 86134 876 2 **ISBN-13** 978 1 86134 876 0

297 x 210mm 64 pages June 2006

Household spending in Britain
What can it teach us about poverty?
Mike Brewer, Alissa Goodman and Andrew Leicester

Much of the recent policy debate surrounding poverty in Britain focuses on income as a measure of living standards. In this report we consider one alternative to income for measuring poverty that has been largely overlooked in the mainstream poverty debate in the UK: namely household expenditure.

Economic theory suggests that household expenditure is an important measure of financial well-being. Using 30 years of data from household surveys, this report:

• shows the trends in poverty in Britain since the 1970s when household expenditure is used as a measure of financial well-being, rather than household income;
• investigates how using spending, rather than income, as a measure of well-being alters our view of who is poor;
• examines the spending levels of the lowest-income households;
• analyses whether low-income pensioners' spending on basic and non-basic items increased as a result of the large increases in entitlements to means-tested benefits since 1999.

Paperback £12.95 US$25.95

ISBN-10 1 86134 854 1 **ISBN-13** 978 1 86134 854 8

297 x 210mm 48 pages April 2006

Free pdf versions available online at www.jrf.org.uk

Graduates from disadvantaged families
Early labour market experiences
Andy Furlong and Fred Cartmel

While the expansion of Higher Education has resulted in an increase in the numbers of disadvantaged young people attending university, the benefits of participation are unclear. This report focuses on the young people's progress from full-time study into the graduate labour market. It highlights the difficulties they encounter and the different types of employment gained. The authors consider whether the time and money the young people invested in Higher Education has paid off in terms of the standards of education achieved, employment outcomes, and the young people's perceptions of themselves, their careers and their lives in general.

Graduates from disadvantaged families is essential reading for careers advisers, recruitment personnel, and researchers with an interest in Higher Education and the graduate labour market. It will also be valuable reading for academics, practitioners and policy makers in the fields of education, social policy, youth and labour market studies.

Two earlier reports, also published by The Policy Press, are *Losing out? Socioeconomic disadvantage and experience in further and higher education* (2003) and *Socioeconomic disadvantage and access to higher education* (2000).

Paperback £12.95 US$25.95

ISBN-10 1 86134 780 4 **ISBN-13** 978 1 86134 780 0

297 x 210mm 56 pages October 2005

The persistence of poverty across generations
A view from two British cohorts
Jo Blanden and Steve Gibbons

The recent focus on reducing the extent of child poverty in the UK stems mainly from worries about the future consequences of poverty on children's later achievement. With this background in mind, it is clearly crucial to improve our understanding of the costs of growing up poor. This report explores the strength of the link between childhood poverty and poverty later in life, and asks whether this link has grown stronger or weaker in recent decades.

This report uses information on the incomes of two British cohorts to address the following questions:

• How large is the transmission of poverty between a teenager's parents' circumstances and their own circumstances when they are in their early 30s?
• By how much has the strength of this transmission of poverty changed between the two cohorts that were teenagers in the 1970s and the 1980s?
• How far do the effects of early disadvantage continue to be felt as individuals reach middle age?

This report will be of interest to policy makers and academics who are concerned with understanding the factors that shape the life-chances of poor children.

Paperback £12.95 US$25.95

ISBN-10 1 86134 852 5 **ISBN-13** 978 1 86134 852 4

297 x 210mm 64 pages April 2006

Free pdf versions available online at www.jrf.org.uk

Economic segregation in England
Causes, consequences and policy
Geoffrey Meen, Kenneth Gibb, Jennifer Goody, Thomas McGrath and Jane Mackinnon

The recent focus on reducing the extent of child One of the key objectives of government neighbourhood policy is to encourage a sustainable mix of tenures and incomes. This report addresses questions of why integration has been so difficult to achieve in practice and draws conclusions for future policy.

The report analyses data from three related empirical studies. The first models, locally, the links between housing, labour markets, migration, deprivation and segregation. The second examines the factors behind the individual moving decisions that lie at the heart of segregation and how policy can influence choices. The third presents three case studies. These are the first empirical studies of their kind to show how segregation and deprivation arise.

Economic segregation in Britain is aimed at policy practitioners, economists and academics working in the fields of housing and neighbourhood revitalisation. Although the report deals with technical modelling issues, it is written in a style accessible to the non-specialist.

Paperback £12.95 US$25.95

ISBN-10 1 86134 813 4 **ISBN-13** 978 1 86134 813 5

297 x 210mm 80 pages December 2005

To order further copies of this publication or any other Policy Press titles please visit **www.policypress.org.uk** or contact:

In the UK and Europe:
Marston Book Services, PO Box 269, Abingdon,
Oxon, OX14 4YN, UK
Tel: +44 (0)1235 465500
Fax: +44 (0)1235 465556
Email: direct.orders@marston.co.uk

In the USA and Canada:
ISBS, 920 NE 58th Street, Suite 300, Portland,
OR 97213-3786, USA
Tel: +1 800 944 6190 (toll free)
Fax: +1 503 280 8832
Email: info@isbs.com

In Australia and New Zealand:
DA Information Services,
648 Whitehorse Road Mitcham,
Victoria 3132, Australia
Tel: +61 (3) 9210 7777
Fax: +61 (3) 9210 7788
E-mail: service@dadirect.com.au

Further information about all of our titles can
be found on our website.

JOSEPH ROWNTREE
FOUNDATION